MW00609695

ANATOMY OF A FRIENDSHIP

A Dual Memoir of Women's Journeys
Through War to Peace

Cherry
Orchard
Books

ANATOMY OF A FRIENDSHIP

A Dual Memoir of Women's Journeys Through War to Peace

Cecile Spiegel and Diane Tuckman

BOSTON
2022

Library of Congress Cataloging-in-Publication Data

Names: Spiegel, Cecile, 1915-2010, author. | Tuckman, Diane, 1935- author.
Title: Anatomy of a friendship : a dual memoir of women's journeys through
    war to peace / Cecile Spiegel and Diane Tuckman.
Description: Boston : Cherry Orchard Books, an imprint of Academic Studies
    Press, 2022.
Identifiers: LCCN 2022001468 (print) | LCCN 2022001469 (ebook) | ISBN
    9781644698358 (hardback) | ISBN 9781644698365 (paperback) | ISBN
    9781644698372 (adobe pdf) | ISBN 9781644698389 (epub)
Subjects: LCSH: Spiegel, Cecile, 1915-2010. | Tuckman, Diane, 1935- |
    Jewish women--United States--Biography. | Women refugees--United
    States--Biography. | World War, 1939-1945--Refugees--Biography. |
    Religious refugees--Germany--Biography. | Religious
    refugees--Egypt--Biography. | Women immigrants--United
    States--Biography. | Female friendship--United States.
Classification: LCC E184.36.W64 S65 2022 (print) | LCC E184.36.W64
    (ebook) | DDC 305.48/892400922 [B]--dc23/eng/20220207
LC record available at https://lccn.loc.gov/2022001468
LC ebook record available at https://lccn.loc.gov/2022001469

ISBN 9781644698358 (hardback)
ISBN 9781644698365 (paperback)
ISBN 9781644698372 (adobe pdf)
ISBN 9781644698389 (epub)

Copyright © 2022, Academic Studies Press
All rights reserved.

Book design by Lapiz Digital Services
Cover design by Ivan Grave. On the front cover: silk paintings by Diane
Tuckman, "Family" (left) and "Tree of Life" (right)

Published by Cherry Orchard Books, an imprint of Academic Studies Press
1577 Beacon Street
Brookline, MA 02446, USA
press@academicstudiespress.com
www.academicstudiespress.com

Contents

Introduction

When we met, Cecile and I were immigrants and housewives living near Washington, DC, in the turbulent 1960s. Cecile's children were grown; mine were toddlers. Ready to pursue work outside the home, we were attracted to teaching jobs that would allow us to use a skill we had in common: we both spoke fluent French. In fact, we both regarded it as our primary language, even though we had acquired and mastered many others along the way. Our shared language and circumstances of fate nudged us toward a friendship that endured forty-five years.

Seeking certification to become teachers of French, we found our separate ways to a training program tailored for native speakers at the University of Maryland, College Park. Most of our classmates were from French-speaking countries.

In class, we were quite the pair: Cecile was the charismatic one with an unexpectedly firm persuasiveness for someone so petite. Her impeccable French was only occasionally betrayed by a slight German accent, her first language. I grew up in Egypt, speaking French, English, Arabic, and Hebrew. Today, I dart between rapid-fire French and English, and my friends say I remain Cecile's emotional and artistic opposite: poised, but always prone to bursts of drama.

First impressions are funny. Cecile said she thought I was arrogant and flamboyant, but admired my confidence and work ethic. I noticed Cecile's reserved elegance, maternal nature, and quick smile. It didn't take long to discover that we shared more than French.

Though we were born almost two decades apart and on different continents, our life stories divide into an incredibly similar series of before-and-after chapters. Before the war. After we fled. Before we married. After we had children. Before we moved to America. After we met.

Our earliest memories are of comforts that we took for granted. Cecile's are set in Nuremberg, in the 1920s and 1930s, while Hitler was rising to power. I was born in Heliopolis, a suburb of Cairo in 1935.

Nowadays, we struggle to remember dates, but just ask us to name favorite tastes or smells from our childhoods! We can instantly summon them, as if they'd been absorbed through our skin and permeated our very identities: pretzels and *metwurst*, a smoked sausage. Spices in the bazaar. Mother's potted jasmine tree.

Looking back now, we are grateful for the love and family stability that our parents provided. These came with generous helpings of Jewish tradition and values. They inoculated us with a sense of heritage that would never be dislodged. Not even by the forces of hatred festering beyond our walls and our parents' control; not by efforts to assimilate us into other cultures when, to protect us from persecution, they prepared us to leave our homelands.

One of the common threads of our lives is our connection to Paris. Cecile arrived first, as a bride-to-be, on the eve of World War II. As Germany's bombs

Diane Tuckman, artist, wearing one of her hand-painted scarves

rained on the capital's suburbs, she joined the throng moving south, seeking a haven where she could bear her first son. Fear, courage, luck, and quick wits mark her story of escaping the Nazi invasion, and her facility with languages helped her pass undetected through many dangerous encounters.

My family arrived in Paris after the war, in 1948, and I recall using ration tickets. Though only a teenager, I was old enough to recognize my parents' sacrifice, and feel guilty that I resented the changes imposed on me. They traded down from a cozy middle-class lifestyle when they became refugees to escape religious persecution in Egypt. Make do with what you have, my parents urged me.

Years later, when opportunities to live in the United States beckoned, Cecile and I both leaped. Arriving in America presented the chance to assess our wanderings and remake, yet again, our futures. Cecile's odyssey had already taken her from Germany to France, and mine from Egypt to France. Perhaps we could abandon some of the cargo that we had borne in our hearts as we crossed the Atlantic. Would we find, at last, a permanent home?

For a very long time, it was convenient to ignore the past and busy ourselves making a future for our own children. Education, husbands, synagogue, community, careers, social lives—day-to-day activities took precedence over other concerns. We can honestly say we have lived what many would call the American Dream.

So why retrace our steps now?

We are not content to fix our eyes only on the horizons of our children's futures or our suburban retirement and elder years. Memories have a way of intruding upon the present and demanding to be acknowledged. Collecting and writing our stories has become a way to honor our parents and those others who took risks so that we could come this far. Also, it is our gift to our grandchildren and their future children, especially to the girls. We want them to know more than the history they will find in textbooks: we want them to know stories of pluck and fortitude as lived by women in their own families.

This may sound simplistic, but it means so much: our legacies are not determined only by the history thrust upon us, but by the choices we make in response. We witnessed that lesson repeatedly during our respective journeys as daughters, sisters, wives, mothers, and friends. As women, aren't we blessed with unique attributes for persevering through the moonless nights of uncertain fate? When at last dawn breaks, there will be wounds to dress and babies to feed and peace to negotiate so that communities can again flourish. No matter which role we play—whether social, political, military, or commercial—we are the ones who will be counted on to serve as bearers of the culture. That's why women's interpretations of history should be treasured!

Cecile Spiegel, in 2007

Our memoir is also our tribute to the power of women's friendships. Thank God we did not have to travel alone on the trip to these cobweb-covered recollections. In our lives, friendship has been the antidote to the aches of otherness, homelessness, and loss that stalk the refugee and immigrant. Revisiting those feelings required a sanctuary that we found in our friendship. Coaxing and encouraging one another, we trudged on, shouldering each other's burdens and marking the milestones. For several years, we interviewed each other (in French, of course), prying and prodding and making a fuss over both the most ordinary and remarkable of reminiscences.

Only a true friend would indulge in such an interrogation! At least we could look forward to soothing our ruffled feathers with homemade soup and a spoonful of Nutella at the end of the day. We wish for every reader the gift of such a friend.

—Diane Tuckman, 2010
Lanham, MD

1

Beginnings / Diane

I hail from Heliopolis, Egypt. I was born there in 1935. Heliopolis is known as the birthplace of the ancient cult of Re, the sun god. In Egyptian mythology, each time it was reborn, the Phoenix brought the ashes of its predecessor to the altar of the sun god at Heliopolis. To know the tale of the Phoenix is to understand something of the life of the refugee and immigrant. She must remake herself again and again during sojourns in foreign lands, amid new languages and unfamiliar customs, while discovering and preserving the essence of her own identity. This is my family's story.

My parents, Esther and Isaac Yedid (which means beloved or friend in Hebrew), were born in Egypt. Isaac's parents, Aslan Yedid and Rachel, were originally from Aleppo, Syria. Esther's mother, Helene Abulafia, was originally from Izmir, Turkey; and her father Isaac Cohen, who was born in Jerusalem, moved to Algeria to find work and there became a French citizen. Our ancestors gathered in Egypt from various parts of the Mediterranean, and in their wanderings came to strengthen the Egyptian Jewish Sephardic community.

For thirty-two centuries, Jews have lived in Egypt, as shown on papyruses and documents found in the genizah (a storage space for sacred and important papers) in the wall of the synagogue in Fostat, Old Cairo. This presence can be seen also in paintings on the walls of ancient synagogues in Cairo, Alexandria, and Mansoura. Paintings on the wall of the tombs of Beni Hasan (from about 2000 BC to 1800 BC) show the arrival of the Jews in Egypt.

The impact of the Jews over the centuries has been profound. In recent times, they played a major part in the modernization of the country. The institutions they promoted include schools, hospitals, and philanthropic organizations, and they are associated with higher education and publishing.

It is said that some Jews actually remained in Egypt at the time of the Exodus. By the twentieth century, this community consisted of more than one hundred thousand individuals and boasted spectacular synagogues, beautiful liturgy, and had contributed to every aspect of Egyptian society, particularly business.

When I was a child, there was a Jewish quarter in the old part of Cairo. I am the second child in my family. My sister Gisele, my parents' first child, was a beautiful girl with lovely curly blond hair and a cheerful disposition. A very caring and wonderful person, she became the matriarch of the family, watching over all of us, giving good advice, and scolding us when necessary. *Une vraie Mère Poule!* Gisele died in 2021.

My father was very interested in everything British; so, when I was born, he decided to name me Diane, instead of a name with origins in our family's heritage or original languages. My nickname was Didi—I do not remember why.

My mother had a very difficult time while pregnant with me, and when I finally arrived I was dark and shriveled. In true Middle Eastern tradition, all the family and friends came to visit. This, of course, is hearsay, but I believe that they all said, "Poor Esther, a second daughter— [meaning no son!]—and she is so ugly!" My parents would hear none of it, and from what I understand, they treated me with great care. And, anyway, my appearance at birth did not last very long. They cherished each one of their children, loved us all, and were very protective. After me came my brother Alain (finally a boy!—and who now looks like a movie star), then my sister Joyce with her shock of curly black hair, finally my brother, easygoing Danny.

My father was from an intellectual, well-to-do family in Syria. His father's first wife (whose name we do not recall) bore a son, Selim, my father's half-brother. Selim eventually moved to Belgium. (His daughter, my cousin Gilberte, sought out the family many years ago. When she found my father, they became fast friends, a mutual admiration society. So, we now have a branch of the family in Belgium which we are in contact with.) After his first wife passed away, my grandfather married her sister Rachel, whom he described as "the love of his life," and they had four children—two boys and two girls. My father was the eldest of that group.

Going to school in those days in Syria was a tricky proposition for a Jewish family. Public schools were out of the question, but in our tradition, a good education was essential. It was also quite expensive. My father and uncles attended a Jesuit school and my aunts went to a convent school, but none participated in the school's religious events.

When my grandmother passed away, my grandfather died shortly after— from a broken heart, it is said. Their four children suddenly became orphans. A wealthy uncle had an apartment in Egypt, where he installed Isaac and his siblings. Then he brought their paternal grandmother (my great-grandmother, whose name we do not remember; it's lost in the mist of time) from Aleppo to help. She taught the two girls how to cook and keep house.

Isaac and his brother were encouraged to acquire a trade. Once they secured clerical jobs, the grandmother decided to go home because she was getting old and wanted to die in her country, where a daughter lived. Isaac, at age fourteen or fifteen, was assigned the job of traveling with her, so she could safely get back home. They went by boat to Damascus, and someone from her family met them there and took charge of getting her to Aleppo, her hometown. My father related to us that he then crossed the desert by bus and train and returned to Egypt. Traveling was certainly not easy in those days, especially for a young person all alone.

The Jewish community in Cairo said they would help place the four children, but that it would be almost impossible to find a family who would take all four; they would have to split them up. My father and his brother adamantly refused. Upon his return from taking his grandmother to Syria, my father became the de facto head of the family. At the ages of fifteen and fourteen, my father and his brother went to work to support and keep them all together. They succeeded. All four were very close for the remainder of their lives, caring and looking after each other as best they could.

My grandmother on my mother's side, Helene Abulafia, was born in Izmir, Turkey, in 1869. It seems that things were difficult, as it was necessary for a young woman to have a dowry in order to attract a husband; but she did not have one. So, she and her sister moved to Cairo to find husbands, because at that time Egypt was an open country with no restrictions in this regard.

There she met and married Isaac Cohen. He was born in Jerusalem. As I mentioned, to find work he later moved to Algeria, which was then a French colony, and therefore he became a French citizen before eventually moving to Cairo. It appears that he owned land and farms in Egypt. He traveled to the farms to see that the fields were planted and properly maintained and harvested. In 1916, coming back from one of those trips, he was robbed during the night and he jumped out of the window to escape the robbers, had a heart attack, and died. He was forty-two years old.

That made my grandmother Helene a widow quite young, left to care for their four children. There were two girls and two boys. My mother, Esther, was nine when he died. In order to support her family, Helene started a design house, as she was very talented in design, sewing, and embroidering. In time, my mother found work in a stationery store in Cairo to help support the family. That is where she met my father.

Esther's brother, who was the oldest son, was my uncle Raphael; he eventually lived in Heliopolis. My aunt Victorine lived in Cairo and, following in her mother's footsteps, was a very talented textile artist. She worked for the Egyptian government and launched a well-respected school to teach textile arts to young women. My grandmother eventually lived with her. My mother, Esther, was the third child. We know very little about the younger brother, Jacques, who enlisted in the French army during WWI. He was awarded a medal by the French government for his service.

Helene is the only one of my grandparents I got to know. She lived with my aunt in Cairo and occasionally came to our home to visit; but we visited them often. She sat cross-legged on the day bed in the girls' room. She would comb her long white hair and make it up into a neat chignon. She wore scarab earrings and simple dresses.

My grandmother spoke mostly Ladino, the language of the Jews who were expelled from Spain in 1492—a blend of Hebrew, Spanish, Turkish, and other Mediterranean influences acquired as they migrated. We spoke French and English at home and Arabic in other places, but very little Ladino, so it was difficult to communicate with her.

Eventually, my grandmother became very sick, and during the last days of her life she was transferred from my aunt's house to our apartment in Heliopolis. I remember that she was placed on a bed in my parents' room. My older sister and I would sneak in to peer at her when no one was looking. My mother had learned to give injections during WWII, so she tended to our grandmother to administer painkillers. I remember the doctors coming in and out and shaking their heads. When she passed away in 1946, they all said it was a blessing as the cancer had invaded her body from her stomach and the pain would have been unbearable. This was my first confrontation with death. I was eleven at that time.

My mother, Esther, was smart, tall, beautiful, always beautifully dressed, and talented in every way: sewing, cooking, charity work, and directing the household. She swam and played basketball—and because she was tall, the center position on the team was always reserved for her.

She looked after us herself and did not delegate the raising of her (five!) children to servants, as upper-class women did then. She viewed it as her primary responsibility, and took no guff from any of us. She was a very busy woman with a strong maternal ethic. This kind of rubbed off on me. We had a good relationship as we struggled through all our peregrinations.

While working at the stationery store, my mother was engaged to a young man (name unknown); he put a ring on her finger. My father walked in one day and it was just like *Le Coup de Foudre*. She attempted to return the ring to her fiancé but he refused to accept it! This ring is now a family heirloom. It is a round medium-sized diamond set in white gold with yellow gold around it. A simple period piece.

So, my parents married, as my father Isaac had by then managed to establish himself in business and could support a family. One of his sisters, who was still single, moved in with them. My mother always said that she knew up front that when she married my father she was also marrying his brother and sisters!

Esther Yedid, Diane's mother

My parents were quite close but they were not very demonstrative. They showed each other respect in speech and action. Also, they were very progressive for their time and we were brought up in a very European, intellectual style, always open to new ideas, some of which my father brought back from his business travels.

Once, he came home with a Victrola phonograph. For the Victrola, he brought only opera records. Talk about censorship! He said we had to learn how to appreciate something we knew nothing about. So, we wound it up and music filled our apartment. I am still not crazy about opera, but my ears can pick out a well-known aria or overture from famous operas. (This later played a great role in my relationship with Cecile, because she was very knowledgeable about classical music and opera. All she needs is to hear a few introductory notes and she can name the opera. On the other hand, I appreciate the pageantry, the costumes, and some of the music, all in a limited way.) On another trip to Europe,

Danny, Joyce, Alain, Diane, and Gisele with parents at El Andalus, a garden park on the Nile in Cairo.

my father brought some classical music records. We liked several of them and played them over and over until we were told to stop because it would wear them out! We all loved the challenge of carefully placing the phonograph needle exactly where it needed to go to avoid damaging the needle or the record.

Living in a cosmopolitan environment, my parents always looked for opportunities to give all of us valuable cultural experiences. Our parents took us to many historical places in Cairo, such as museums and cultural sites, so I gained an early appreciation for art. One time, after a business trip, my father came back with a Morris car. That changed our life in many ways.

Our parents gave us the opportunity to take ballet classes. They selected a delightful lady from London, England, to instruct us in her studio in the suburbs where we lived. She was four feet eight inches tall with a very strong personality. She had danced with the Royal Ballet in London and was quite experienced. She was a strict disciplinarian, particularly when we advanced and started taking pointe. Everything had to be done just so. She was a stickler for all the details so we would not get injured: how to prepare the shoes with the toe protectors, how to lace them up properly, and how to approach every step. We really looked forward to each class. As kids, my sister Gisele and I loved ballet! We always felt like we were reaching for the stars, particularly when on pointe.

Ballet classes were among the first things eliminated when it became dangerous for us to navigate the streets. It was heartbreaking.

My father was always in business on his own, as he had learned early in life to fend for himself. He liked it that way. He was in the import-export business, was the agent, and represented different companies; he traveled extensively. He spoke several languages and that was a great asset in his business dealings. He was fearless and good at what he did.

I still have a woolen scarf made from tartan samples from a company he represented. It was two short pieces so we stitched them together, overlocked the edges, and added black wool fringe, which we hand knotted at both ends.

Later, after moving to Canada, he became the agent for Larousse, the famous French publishing house, and sold their books, particularly children's books, in the Quebec hinterlands. Always open to new things, when he went to Italy and came across the brown tape which is now a staple all over the world, he immediately saw the potential and became the manufacturer's representative in Canada for a while. On a trip to France, he discovered the Cuisinart (an American-made electric food processor created in the 1970s). He did not manage to have a business connection with them, but my mother had a Cuisinart before anybody else we knew. He eventually represented a famous French company that manufactured exquisite knitting wools, Chat Botté.

My parents were generally in good health most of their lives. My father never went to a doctor until his first heart episode in his sixties. While he was in the hospital, the doctor mentioned to him that smoking was not a good idea. He went cold turkey that day. My brothers and younger sister who lived at home also smoked. Leading by example, he encouraged them all to stop. They eventually did. We did not know about secondhand smoke at the time.

Although he had a heart condition, he remained healthy, shunning doctors and medications when possible. I remember when the doctor told him to stop using salt. When people asked him how he could do it, his comment was: "So, what is wrong with pepper?" When he could no longer drive, he would say: "What is wrong with buses and cabs?" Contemporaries would fret: "It's expensive to take cabs." His response was: "Maintaining a car is expensive and what did you save money for, to become a prisoner in your own house?" He was always on the go, even in the cold Montreal winters. He audited courses at McGill University. As he walked on campus, his grandchildren, who were students there, would point him out to friends. Once he walked into the classroom; the teacher stopped teaching because his stories were so interesting to the students. He attended services at the synagogue and ran errands. He walked to the local stores a few blocks away.

He became depressed when his health started to fail. My sister Gisele helped him get over it. He then said he could not leave (die) before my mother; he had to look after her. At some point she had fallen a few times and was in terrible pain. She made every single one of us promise not to place her in a nursing home. When she got sick, she refused to go to the doctor. She was treated for back pain. Eventually the pain got so bad that my brother Danny persuaded a doctor friend to make a house call. The doctor took one look at her and she was immediately sent to the hospital. It turned out that she had cancer. She died ten days later. My father went into the hospital with a heart problem while she was going downhill, but he recovered and went home. He eventually got sick again and went to the hospital.

The day my mother passed away, my sister Gisele and my brother Alain went to tell him. When they arrived at the hospital he was crying. He said, "You do not need to tell me, I know she died last night." He survived her by thirty-six days.

We all returned to Montreal for a second funeral shortly after the first one.

In 1947, Hakoah club visited Aboukir, Egypt, site of a former Royal Air Force base. Diane is at center, second row from top.

What Cannot Be Taken Away from You

My childhood had all the hallmarks of privilege: maids, membership of a private club, and good schools; connections to French and British groups that were considered prestigious; a Westernized education, ballet, music, and activities with the Hakoah, the Jewish Youth movement.

Education was a very strong value. My father said, "If you do not use your head you will have to use your feet." My parents also said, "They can take everything away from you except Education, with a capital E, so go for it, be it formal or informal."

I find it interesting that this came from my parents, who due to the fact that they both lost parents early, did not have the opportunity to attend college. Yet, wherever they went, they were always considered wise and smart. They had common sense and were self-educated. They always sought knowledge and applied it to their daily lives.

I took their advice to heart. Reading was my escape. I could travel in books, use them as a path to continuing education. With three siblings sleeping in one room and frequently wanting to finish a book, reading under the covers with a flashlight was a common occurrence. During the hard times, our entertainment was sitting around the table and discussing the books we had read from the free library, such as French literature, philosophy, Jewish topics, etc. . . .

I was introspective as a child. NO DOLLS for me! I was more of an intellectual. I liked to talk to adults and learn things from them. My father was a great fan of Maimonides, one of the great Jewish minds of medieval times and who had lived and practiced as a physician in Cairo. Maimonides was very active in responsa during his time. That is the mechanism through which great Jewish scholars communicated and discussed issues and gave their opinions. In essence, they responded to queries. One of my aunts, my father's sister Alice, worked at the orphanage in the Cairo Jewish Quarter next door to the place where Maimonides had taught and practiced medicine. My father worked close by. To think that I walked the same streets as Maimonides and many other famous Jews blows my mind.

When Gisele and I were ready to go to school, our parents enrolled us in the Jewish day school, next to the synagogue in Heliopolis. Within a couple of days, we came home with aching knuckles. The teacher had used a ruler to discipline us for making mistakes. The next day we were taken out of that school. As my father put it, "No one will lay a hand on my children!" He was well ahead of his time.

My parents sat us down and told us we would instead attend English Mission College, a Christian institution. Our parents believed the goal of this school was to convert its students; their own goal, they said, was to expose us to other religions, and they made it crystal clear to the school and to us that we had to maintain our faith.

At English Mission College we had Bible class, but we were exempt from participating in any religious activity, even Christmas events. Our parents had negotiated this well in advance before they registered us. We were not the only ones, as other Jewish and Muslim families sent their children to this good school. My parents explained that we would get our Jewish classes somewhere else, at Abraham Betesh, the equivalent of a Jewish religious school, named after its founder/patron. That is where we learned Hebrew and the traditions.

At English Mission College, we learned to speak English with a British accent—as it was a requirement. American English was not acceptable. While we were in the playground, there were prefects around; when they heard us speak American English, we got demerits. We also studied French and Arabic. Studying Arabic was mandatory regardless of what school we were in.

Meanwhile, my three younger siblings attended the Lycée Francais.

We spoke French and English at home and Arabic on the street and with the maids. Today, people frequently ask me if I think in English or French. (Cecile was frequently in the same position.) Well, I think in both languages

Diane's teachers at the English Mission College in Egypt

and it alternates depending on the situation. This sometimes leads to utter confusion. My speech gets garbled as I search for the right words to express my thoughts. I warn my family, friends, and silk-art students, to question me when they do not understand what I have just said. I speak English and French very well, but despite the fact that I went to French schools for several years, writing French is now altogether another story as I left France in 1958. I have found that saying a telephone number in French is difficult. Several other people have told me they have the same problem. I do not understand why. As for Arabic, well, having not had a chance to speak it at all for several years, I do not speak it at all, understand only a few words during a conversation, and certainly cannot read it. I can still read liturgical Hebrew.

One of my childhood teachers from England was so enamored with New Zealand that she imparted that obsession to me. She always inspired me to broaden my horizons and expand my outlook. It was one of my goals to visit New Zealand and to confirm the stories she had so vividly described. And, indeed, I did. At some point later in life, when I moved to America, I realized it was "now or never." So, I organized a trip to New Zealand, Australia, and New Guinea. It was all that she had described, and then some. The trip was very exciting and educational, and full of adventures, such as going down the rapids in a boat . . .

On the campus was a wide sunny room, which used to be a greenhouse. It was transformed into an art room because of the extensive view of the gardens—the flowers, the plants, the insects. I specifically remember seeing several praying mantises climbing up the glass. I consider it a good introduction to art: up close.

At English Mission College, you had to wear a uniform. In the cooler months, it was a brown jumper with a belt, a white shirt, and a brown tie. That is where I learned to knot a tie, as I had to do it every morning. In the summer, we wore dresses with a small blue and white floral print and a plain white round collar and belt.

We shopped in the bazaar. I remember the blended smells of spices and a huge array of foods of every description. Once, before WWII, I was in the bazaar with my mother. The street, if you could call it that, was very narrow between the stalls. Huge American cars would come lumbering down with incessantly blowing horns. Suddenly I let out a scream. A wheel on one of these behemoths was on my foot. You never saw such a commotion! The occupants—two corpulent men and the driver—were afraid to move the car as my foot would be crushed. They quickly got out and several bystanders were commandeered to lift the car off my foot. I still have a slight indentation there, but I was really lucky and unharmed!

Religious Life

Vitali Madjar. © 2017 Diarna: The Geo-Museum of North African and Middle Eastern Jewish Life. Photographer: Joshua Shamsi

Our Hebrew school in Heliopolis was adjacent to the synagogue, the Vitali Madjar, on El Missalah street, built in 1928. I recall the synagogue as being a large structure with beautiful stained glass windows, an imposing bimah in the center, and an elaborate ark. The women's section was located on the second floor, with lattice screening to visually separate them from the men.

On the Sabbath, I often went with my father to synagogue. While I was still young, I could sit with him on the main floor. As I grew older, I was constantly questioned about my age by the guys at the door. They always wanted me to retreat to the balcony reserved for women. My father was aware of how I chafed under that rule, and would ask them to let me sit with him as I was still young enough. His seat in the small building faced the doors which opened onto the courtyard. He just took me by the hand with him until it was no longer possible. With no air conditioning and in very hot weather, these doors and the windows opposite them were open for cross-ventilation. We welcomed the breezes. The courtyard was covered with sand. We kids played there and frequently took off our sandals—a great feeling.

Services were quite well attended, but during the holidays it was mayhem, packed with people spilling out onto the sidewalk. People pushed and shoved to get into the small synagogue during the important parts of the services. In the old traditional way, honors were auctioned off during the service. No money was immediately exchanged because it is prohibited to handle money at those points of the worship; the pledged donations were delivered later. Basically, the synagogue was supported by the people who attended.

For family events such as weddings and Bar Mitzvahs, we went to the main synagogue in Cairo, Shaar Hashamayim. On these occasions, tables were set in the courtyard and laden with the food prepared cooperatively by the women in the family. I remember these feasts were amazing in the variety, quality, and quantity of what was prepared.

Then the holidays rolled around. My mother would swing into action, far in advance. I really enjoyed going with my mother to shop for the food and to watch the merchants do their thing. At the market, she chose the live chickens she wanted for the holiday meals. Although we did not keep kosher, my mother would purchase kosher meat and chickens for the holidays. The shochet would quickly and skillfully slit the throats of the chickens in the traditional way, and someone standing nearby would pluck and clean them. We loved to look for eggs inside the chicken. The double-yolk ones were a true prize!

At Passover, pandemonium broke out in the household, with long lists of things to do. One of the corners in the dining room was cleared out to make room for the large, tall, willow basket which contained the delicate, wide matza, which were layered between sheets of paper.

With two maids and my mother working together, cleaning the kitchen was fast work. Next, a clean white sheet covered the table in the dining room, then a huge bag of rice was dumped in the middle. It had to last the entire holiday and feed an army of people. All hands on deck! We sat around the table, scooped some rice towards us, removed any impurities, and then dumped the rice in a bowl. We had a wonderful time chatting, teasing each other and the maids.

After the reading of the Passover story, we all laughed because we were living in Egypt, the land from which our ancestors had escaped. The plate with all the traditional symbols was placed in the center of the table and prayers were recited. Once this part was over, the center plate was removed and a roast leg of lamb was placed in the center of the table to be carved and served. That was not all: the table was then covered with many dishes. Plain boiled eggs and eggs which had been boiled with onion skins so that they turned brown. This was followed by cold fish. We loved the velvety veal meatballs prepared with rice flour and steeped in a delicious sauce. Great over the rice! *Kobebah* made with matza meal, stuffed artichokes, and always rice. Green beans were the usual vegetable, as well as tomatoes and cucumbers. During all that time, we reached over to the large basket and pulled out the delicate matzas.

Once we'd staggered through all this wonderful food, the table was cleared off again and the desserts appeared. Sponge cake, an assortment of cookies, dates stuffed with almonds, pistachios, assorted nuts, and of course fresh fruit. The exquisite desserts my mother baked for the holiday were a real treat. I am still looking for some of these recipes. We always had bowls of the traditional haroset made with dates and the popular coconut jam.

During the week-long holiday many other delicacies were prepared. A favorite was layers of hard matza, soaked in broth, layered with ground meat and pine nuts, and baked. Sometimes spinach was used.

For the holidays we frequently visited relatives and friends or they came to see us. Sweets and savory goodies were generously proffered. The High Holy days were more subdued, but still quite busy. During Hannukah, we went to visit relatives and friends and the usual goodies were offered. The children were given coins to symbolize the holiday.

At Home

I can still remember the landscape of my childhood: the apartment, the cool floors, the streets. As we walked down the streets, we frequently passed young kids who were bedraggled, dirty, and covered with flies. It was very difficult for me to see that, because my parents emphasized cleanliness. It really broke my heart and made me very sad to see these young children in such a bad situation.

I felt then, and still do, that we were privileged, because we lived in a spacious apartment, tastefully furnished with two live-in maids. Our home was modest by many standards: it had three large bedrooms, a small living room, a dining room, kitchen, and a bathroom. In the back of the apartment were two bedrooms, one for the boys and one for the girls. My parents' bedroom was in the front. This is where a sick child got to spend the night in their very large bed. When I caught pneumonia, I spent several days there while recovering. Penicillin had just come out on the market. (We also had to learn how to deal with common diseases in Egypt. The biggest scare was confronting a serious outbreak of cholera.)

All three bedrooms had large cupboards for our clothes. I particularly remember the one in the boys' room because it was a beautiful shade of blue, as well as the one in my parents' bedroom made of acajou. These bedrooms were important because we spent a fair amount of time there.

Adjacent to my parents' bedroom and off the dining room was a large square veranda. There, my mother had several plants in pots, including a fragrant jasmine tree. That is where the entire family gathered in the evening, when the sun had set and the breezes started to cool things down. We frequently ate on the veranda, in the dark, with the scent of jasmine wafting around us. The maids gladly kept us company and visitors frequently joined in. The yogurt salad, which was frequently served as a side dish, was a favorite. Chunks of ice were placed into the yogurt as well as peeled, sliced, tiny fresh pickling cucumbers, garlic, mint, salt, and pepper. Small sweet pastries and fruit were also served.

There was also a narrower balcony off the living room and one along the two bedrooms in the back. These were important features because they created cross-ventilation.

I recall a story of an incident involving my brother Alain. He is a very determined person. On a specific occasion, my parents went to an event and left the maids in charge of all five of us. Alain was particularly obnoxious that day, and we lured him onto the longer balcony and locked the two doors and trapped him out there. He kept banging on the doors, demanding to be let in. We simply taunted him from the inside. He got so infuriated that he slammed his wrist through one of the windows. His artery was severed and the blood came pouring out. We were all in shock. The maids somehow managed to get help very quickly and he was saved.

Due to the intense heat and humidity in the middle of the day, everyone took a long nap. And if one could not sleep, whispering and reading were acceptable substitutes as resting was imperative. One day, during nap time, we could not find my brother Danny anywhere. We eventually located him lying on the terrazzo floor to stay cool under the bed...

The furniture in the small living room was light and airy. I remember a lovely glass cocktail table. A beautiful glass bowl was always placed in the center and frequently filled with scented flowers. Every Friday the bowl was refilled.

The all-white-tiled bathroom contained a large-footed tub. We were all scrubbed in there every day.

Along the corridor, where the icebox was located, were windows facing onto the square, very small, inner courtyard. The corridor windows went all the way up to the top of the building to help create a cross-current. This is where we huddled on pillows, on the floor, during air raids in WWII. I particularly remember how the raids grew more intense during the Battle of El-Alamein (about 150 miles west of Cairo), where British forces repelled General Erwin Rommel and the German and Italian drive into Egypt in 1942. All the windows were covered with black fabric during the air raids.

Our apartment was on the top floor with access to the roof above us. All the kids loved the roof! We could see quite far because there was a racetrack across the street, one building away, which opened up the vista. It was a little far but we could watch the races from our roof. During the war, the British were bivouacked in the middle of the racetrack.

We enjoyed running through the linens and clothes hung on the roof to dry. It was a large space to play, except during the middle of the day in the hot blazing sun.

On that same roof were two more rooms. The maids lived in one and the doorkeeper, his lovely young wife, and two children lived in the other. He was an old man in his seventies and she was quite young. We always thought that was quite strange. My mother felt sorry for her, believing she would end up being a young widow with no one to care for her and the children. Maman taught her how to knit and embroider, and many other skills which might serve her well in later years when she would need to care for her children.

My mother was very caring this way and looked out for everyone around her, a trait which my sister Gisele acquired.

We three girls had to learn how to do everything. We kept saying we would marry rich husbands. When we complained about having sometimes to clean the bathroom, my parents would tell us that we would someday need to know everything because one never knows in life; a rich husband is not always in the cards, they would say. Well, all that good advice and training sure came in handy later, as they were proven right. Learning to sew, embroider, and knit was considered very important. They certainly were excellent skills which helped us through the difficult times when our circumstances changed. When I started a business and hired young people to help, I would always ask them to clean the bathroom. They would look at me wide-eyed in disbelief! But I would say, "You have to know how to do everything!"

On our street, the vendors loudly publicized their wares and we children were sometimes sent down to pick up the goods. Or, because we lived on the third floor, the money was thrown down in packets and the goods left with the porter for later collection. The goats were milked right into our containers!

To the Shore!

When school was over for the year, we were all loaded onto the train for Alexandria, where we spent all summer. Too hot in the city! The historic port city of Alexandria lies about 140 miles northwest of Cairo, on the Mediterranean. My parents rented a small apartment, one block away from Cleopatra Beach. We could even see the beach from one of the balconies. We were crammed in there at night along with the maids. It was hot until the late evening breezes cooled things down. My father went back and forth to his office in Cairo, as he had to work. In the morning we got into our bathing suits and headed for the beach. Breakfast, lunch, and dinner were brought to the beach by the maids. We never left until it was cool and dark, just in time to get to bed. There were cabins for rent on the beach. We never rented one, because we were so close to the apartment.

Diane's family at Cleopatra Beach, Alexandria, Egypt

We would frequently get sunburned, and when we got back to the apartment, the maids would prepare a mixture of water and starch and place it on our backs. As it dried, it would flake off and it itched when we slept. We gradually got over the sunburn during the summer.

As we spent so many hours on the beach, one of the activities we all participated in was trying to catch tiny colorful fish in the crevasses of the rocks when the tide was low. We kept them in small containers for a few hours to admire them, then threw them back.

We returned back home to Heliopolis just a week before school started so we could get ready. I remember that one year my mother lost her wedding ring on the beach. Somehow it slipped off her finger. Picture this: the kids, the maids, and my mother, with tears in her eyes, sifting through the sand where she had been standing. It was to no avail. It is still in the sand of Cleopatra Beach in Alexandria . . .

When we were in Alexandria, we were particularly fond of the roasted corn, which vendors prepared right there on their carts. Dried nuts, such as pistachios, were also sold, as were Italian ices, *gazouzas* (carbonated drinks), and fresh lemonade. For a very low price, some vendors also sold prickly pears, which were peeled and placed on ice to keep them fresh and tasty. I never understood how they could remove the thorny skin of the prickly pears with their bare hands.

We also hunted for *ritza*—sea urchins. They are delicious when opened fresh. Lemon is squeezed on the beautiful yellow meat, and then they are gobbled down. We had to really watch out for their thorns, as they were quite painful and difficult to remove from our hands and feet. (Many years later, I visited my friend Colette Gouin in the south of France. She took me to a port with small very colorful boats. They only fish for sea urchins, a specialty of that area, so I got to relish very fresh *ritza* again.)

2

Beginnings / Cecile

Aufgenommen in Bayrischzell 1919

Cecile with parents Ida and Otto Steinhard, visiting Bavaria

I was born in Nuremberg, Germany, in 1915. I was the only child of Ida and Otto Steinhard. They were wonderful parents and I enjoyed a comfortable childhood. My father was a dentist, my mother an accomplished pianist. They adored me

Otto Steinhard

and taught me many terrific life lessons which I cherish and adhere to up to this day.

On my wall is a photograph that shows my mother holding me, an infant on a beautiful lacy pillow. No naked picture of me on a sheepskin in a photographic studio! It appears that the "baby on the lace pillow" pose was also all the rage at the time.

During WWI, my father had served in the army as a dentist and an officer. He looked quite dashing in his uniform. Besides spoiling me, he taught me some of his skills, such as how to prepare bandages, keep wounds clean and disinfected, and how not to panic in general, even when I saw blood. All good lessons. I trained myself to look out during thunderstorms as a way to remain calm and enjoy the natural spectacle, something unusual I do to this day. He was a charming, calm, and cheerful person, conscious of his charisma, which came from his deep self-confidence. He was popular with his family, friends, and patients. I had a good relationship with him. I have his looks and cheerful temperament. He was a handsome sharp dresser and always looked well turned out.

He had a passion for history, geography, and architecture. I recall that every day after lunch (he came home for lunch), he would pull out a huge book about the monuments in Franken and immerse himself in it. He had beautiful reddish-blond wavy hair. I remember him sitting there, reading the book, and running his hand through his hair. This is captured in a photo of him: my father is so dapper, sitting on a chair, impeccably dressed, as he always was, with his tie knotted just so, his shoes with bows and heels, a flower in his lapel. This particular photograph is in poor condition but certainly depicts him well as a confident fellow.

My sweet mother loved to stay home and tend to the household. She went shopping at the famous Nuremberg market every other day. It was a half-hour walk each way. She had to carry all the groceries back in the typical net bags of the time.

She was also very interested in the arts. She played the piano beautifully with great emotion. I spent many happy hours listening to her playing and singing the music of Schubert and other composers. She had a lovely alto voice. This musical talent ran in her family, as her sister Paula was a piano teacher.

On my father's side, it was a different story. He was taking piano lessons at the age of fourteen when the teacher slapped him for making a mistake. He immediately slapped her back and that was the end of his musical training.

My mother's best friend, Ursula, had a beautifully trained opera voice. She looked like what I envisioned to be the perfect opera singer: she had red wavy hair and was quite tall. Unfortunately, on account of a physical leg deformity she could never become a star. My room was next to our music room so I heard them play and sing often. I remember that Ursula also had an exquisite harp, hidden behind the armoire. She never played it and I never asked or knew why. Of course, I do not know what happened to it.

Paula and Ida Lehman, 1914

My parents and Ursula frequently had musical evenings in the living room. I was very interested in music but not permitted to stay up; but my room was adjacent so I vicariously got to attend.

I have a very large photo album which contains photographs from my early childhood and life in Germany until the time I escaped. It has pictures of me from birth on. It is large, heavy and bulky with a red leather cover and gold lettering saying "Cäcilie Else," my name, on the top right corner. My mother had it made for me. (It seems that my aunt Paula, my mother's sister, took the album when she left Germany, and many years later it came back into my possession. I was reunited with it through the family in America. A total miracle!)

Ida (Lehman) Steinhard, Cecile's mother

In my photo album is a portrait of my mother, the talented pianist. She stands in a comfortable fashion pose in her living room. She is a little buxom, with hair piled up high to make her appear taller. The obviously cinched waist indicates a tight girdle underneath. Her floor-length dress with asymmetrical side panel and a flower at the waist reflects her sense of good taste.

It was a family tradition that every Friday my father brought my mother special gifts: a delicious huge chocolate bar with nuts, flowers, and the weekly *Munich Illustriete*, an interesting newspaper with a serial novel which appeared below a bar on the front page. The novel, I remember, was *Studchem Helene Wilfur*, by Vicki Baum. It was the story of a very liberated woman. My mother and I really enjoyed it. The talented writer, who was Jewish, was eventually deported to a concentration camp.

As a child in Nuremberg, I was a picky eater. I did not like any meat, especially *rinderbraten*, a German holiday food. It is beef which is roasted in a special way. It was hard to chew and did not taste very good. I would quietly go to the bathroom to spit it out. My favorite foods were mashed potatoes, schnitzel, and sauerkraut. I particularly liked *auflauf*, a type of soufflé which was light and fluffy.

We had a maid, Christel, who stayed with us for many years. She maintained the house during the week, while the heavy cleaning was done by a weekly maid. Christel also did the cooking. At times I was left in Christel's care, which was a nightmare. She acted out all her frustrations and resentment on me.

Anna started out as a cook with us but quickly became my nanny. She was good natured, loved me, and we got along very well; it was a delight compared to my time with Christel.

When I was six or seven years old, I used to go with my mother to a seamstress. Actually, there were two of them. Once, my mother left me there for a little while. They started talking about the Jews and said many nasty things. I was just a child and felt powerless to say anything. I never forgot this experience.

I always definitely felt that I was Jewish. It was innate. I did not think of it per se; it was a given, ingrained in my soul. In my home we observed the holidays, to the extent that my mother and I went to synagogue on the High Holy days. On Yom Kippur, we fasted for half the day. The synagogue in Nuremberg was large and beautiful with the bema or lectern in front of the ark. The women were in the upper balcony.

Religious education was part of the regular school curriculum. Twice a week, when it was time for religious class, each group went to a separate room. I remember that I constantly challenged the teacher with difficult questions. I was a holy terror. We were taught history and some Hebrew. At the age of fourteen we had a confirmation ceremony.

I attended the synagogue with my friends. While walking there and back, the boys and girls flirted, but we also had many interesting and serious discussions. An older boyfriend once gave me a book, which he dedicated to me: "To the little princess Cecile, to dream on." It inspired me, so I kept it for a long time.

This idyllic life was interrupted in 1929 with the Depression. I was fourteen years old. One million German marks suddenly became one mark!

My father's patients could not afford to pay him, therefore times became very difficult. We had to move from where we lived to Gartenstaat (Garden City), close to a lovely park which was near a canal that wended its way from Nuremberg to Fürth, and that was surrounded by woods on both sides. Quite lovely, but a big step down for us. My father became the dentist for that neighborhood, servicing workers with a health plan. He could only earn a specific maximum amount. Anything over that was lost to him. So he was on a fixed income while working very hard.

Extended Family Ties

My mother's family was closely knit. I dearly loved all my aunts and their spouses, as well as my uncle and his wife. Until the age of fourteen, I spent all my vacations with Uncle Bert Lehman, his wife Hilde, and their three children. My cousins were like brothers and sisters to me, as I was an only child.

Uncle Bert is the individual I have admired the most in my life. He was so capable in everything he pursued. He was good at athletics, languages, and math. I was told that at the age of nine, he went to math classes with eleven-year-olds. He could solve all the problems in his head.

On my father's side, his brother, my uncle Fritz, was a physician with a general practice. He was married and had a son, Walter. While I was still in Germany, we saw them occasionally. His wife Selma had relatives in America so they were able to emigrate to America early on.

Aunt Regina Lehman with Cecile and cousins Edgar, Margot, and Herbert

I went to Wurzburg during the holidays, where my mother's sister Regina lived. She was married but had no children, so I was cherished by she and Ferdinand, her husband. I had several friends there and always had a wonderful time. The boys and girls went for long walks in the country.

On our walks we visited the old "burg," which was a lot of fun. It is a castle with a huge moat which was built in the Middle Ages.

Many years later, I saw it during one of my visits back to Germany. It was like a museum depicting this period in history. From the burg, there was a beautiful view of Nuremberg and the surrounding areas.

Sometimes, I would also visit Munich where my aunt Paula and her husband Ludwig lived, as well as Uncle Bert and his family. Like all the Lehman women, except for my mother, my aunts had no children. They treated me like I was their child. So, these holiday visits were very special for me.

Cecile's Aunt Paula and Uncle Ludwig Kurtzman, who lived in Munich

My aunt's maid, Gerte, and their cook, Senta, were also very fond of me. Senta would take me on walks to hunt for mushrooms so she could incorporate them in the dishes she prepared. I learned from her how to select the safe ones from the poisonous ones.

According to Margot, Cecile's cousin who lives in New York, Cecile and her three cousins, the children of Uncle Bert and Aunt Hilde, were very close. Cecile spent most of the summer with them. She frequently babysat for them. Cecile was extremely fond of her Aunt

Hilde. One summer, Cecile told Uncle Bert that she was getting a five in French. Six is the worst. He said this was unacceptable, so he devised a plan. She was to report to his office every morning and he would tutor her and give her homework. The next day, he tested her, and that continued all summer. When she went back to school, she was earning a grade of two, which is B. She loved the praise from the teachers at school and continued to do well, as she loved to speak French. Her fluency in the language and excellent accent saved her life more than once.

In school, I was quite mischievous, and having fun was most important. That made me very popular because the other kids did not have the courage to do the things I did. My nickname was Mademoiselle Übermut (*übermut* means "devilish or high-spirited" in German).

We had a teacher who was not very popular. One day I decided to play a trick. I dumped her full trash can on her desk. It was a mess! When she arrived, she was furious and immediately asked who had done this. Nobody said anything. She was determined to find out. So, during the day, she gradually went down the list alphabetically and asked each person. Of course, they all said no. Toward the end of the list, at the letter S (Steinhard) it was my turn. I could not lie because my parents had taught me never to lie, so I confessed. The whole class exploded in laughter. Of course, I was severely reprimanded and also had to go to detention. But I did not care.

At school, I was not a good student—I just got by. I did not pay attention and my homework was frequently neglected. Having a good time was my goal.

In my class, about half the students were Jewish. It was not an issue at the time.

Julius Wasserman, My First Love

Dancing lessons for young people were organized by the Jewish community. They took place in private homes on Friday evenings, and our parents paid for them. It was a great way to meet other Jewish youngsters in a social setting.

Around the age of fifteen, I went to dance class. Sometimes, members of the class had private dance parties that went on all night long. It was fun.

In class, dance partners were selected alphabetically. The boys had to pick up the girls at home. We walked to class. They took turns. Julius and I were at the end of the alphabet: Steinhard and Wasserman. He was very shy. He was two years older than I and he attended a different school. He was a very good student and had a broad education because he was so smart, not lazy like me! He was very calm and considerate.

I asked a friend, "What should we talk about?" She immediately said skiing. That was his passion and he was a great skier. He loved to talk about skiing, which I enjoyed. I understand that he could have made the Olympic team if it hadn't been for what was going on in Germany at the time.

In dance class, all the young girls sat there in rows looking pretty and terrified. "What if I am not chosen?" we all thought! And sadly, it happened to some; but, fortunately, not to me. So, one day, Julius picked me out and we became friends.

A wealthy, elegant aunt of mine from America would occasionally send me clothes which were out of style for her. As we were about the same size, they were just perfect. Some of the dresses she sent were wonderful for dances. One of them was an exquisite bright red taffeta dress with a very large bow on the left side. It fit me to a T and I looked grand in it. I was so excited. But . . . that was the ONLY time I was not asked (to dance) by a partner. Why? Julius told me that it was the old-fashioned bow!

Apparently, Julius was not totally discouraged by the red bow. He did not like to dance but I loved it. He liked to play tricks. I was often the brunt of these jokes. I once went to the ladies' room during one of the dances. There was a large scale there and as I was ready to leave, just for the fun of it, I stepped on it. I could not believe how heavy I had gotten! He had snuck in and placed his foot on the scale, and was amused by my shock.

That is how I met my future husband. I gradually realized he was special and the guy for me. It was not sudden. We continued our relationship, realizing it was a good one.

Crisis Foreshadowed

In school, I went on an excursion organized by Verein für das Deutschtum im Ausland, a very rightist organization dedicated to preserving the "Germanness" of the people. During this excursion, it was the first time that I experienced subtle problems about being Jewish. A young man apparently liked me and was walking with me. So I made it a point, right up front, to tell him that I was Jewish. He dropped me like a hot potato. There I was with nobody to walk with. He turned to another girl and everyone had a companion except me.

Most of my life, I was always very quick to tell people I was Jewish. I felt that it was easier to cut them off at the pass and that it was not fair to start a friendship with that fact looming in the background. This is something I do not do now. I prefer to get to know them, let them like me, and at some point "drop the bomb." In my perspective, a friend is a friend. No need to delineate between Jewish and non-Jewish.

One day, in his office, my father suddenly got very sick and collapsed. He had a kidney problem, which he had developed years earlier while he was in the army. He was rushed to Wurzburg, a city that had a good medical facility, as it was a university town. But he was very sick and could not be saved. My father died in 1932 at the age of fifty-two. His poor health and intense hard work contributed to his early death.

I was seventeen years old when he died. My mother kept the office open for a year and we stayed in the house where the practice was located. She hired a woman dentist and got a percentage of the fees. Once the year was over, the practice, along with the house, was sold to the woman and we moved to our former neighborhood in Nuremberg.

That year (1932), I got a job as an office clerk in a wholesale clothing business in Nuremberg where we were living. The owner was a very kind Jewish man, Mr. Bechhoefer.

One day, a friend came to pick me up from work. While on the street we were stopped by the SA (an abbreviation of Sturmabteilung: Brown Shirts). They confronted us because my friend looked Jewish, which he was, and they accused him of going out with a German girl, me. I immediately told them that I was Jewish, but they did not believe me. They took us upstairs where I worked. When this was confirmed by Mr. Bechhoefer, we were let go.

This was yet another incident which illustrates the political and social climate of that time. The verboten issue! At that time the word *verboten* (forbidden) was everywhere. Forbidden to do this, forbidden to do that. . . . It was very wearing and unnerving.

Sometimes, at work, I had to go upstairs in the area where packages were prepared for shipping. At some point, while there, I suddenly noticed that the conversation hushed when I entered. I wondered why. Then gradually people became more belligerent and unpleasant to me. It then escalated to being told nasty things about Mr. B. I challenged them. They subsequently went and told him that I was the one saying bad things about him. When I heard that, I started to cry, but he consoled me and told me not to pay attention.

In that year, the Nazi problems started in earnest. Upon my mother's advice, I decided to throw my father's pistol in the canal. That was a good move because a few days later they came searching the house for weapons. So, one hurdle was overcome. But because of this event, my mother had a strong nervous reaction and was very distraught. I guess something like a breakdown.

Eventually, things got worse in Nuremberg because it was considered the capital of the Nazi movement. My mother and I were actually living right in the midst of it.

So, I left my job and we moved to Munich where the situation was slightly better, and where Uncle Bert and other family had lived. My address there was 27 Teng Strasse.

Uncle Bert was a banker, extremely knowledgeable about finances. He foresaw the future, and with his family left Germany in 1932, well before the situation seriously deteriorated. He had been to America before and had become an American citizen, and so he settled his family there. He left behind a beautiful house and seven other properties. He placed someone in charge in Munich so that income continued for a while, most likely from rentals. His sisters, Paula, Louise, Regina, and my mother Ida would receive fifteen percent of the income from the properties.

Because my mother and her sisters were part owners, we were given a rent-free apartment in Schwabing. It was a beautiful neighborhood. So, I ended up living close to my cousins Herbert, Edgar, and Margot Lehman, which made me very happy.

The Rise of Hitler

In 1934, my mother decided that it was time for me to leave Germany. There was little fanfare, just a decision: she felt it was best for me.

There was no single, precipitating event. However, she believed that I would be safer outside Germany. She had witnessed the turmoil and momentous changes occurring in German society, and the growing support of the German people for Hitler's propaganda. Her brother, Bert, had already departed for America. She was not ready to leave her homeland, nor could she imagine that her safety would be threatened in her established and comfortable community. Yet she was not willing to gamble on my future.

Just the year before, Adolf Hitler had become chancellor of Germany. He immediately began using the Nazi party to dismantle democracy and impose his antisemitic and nationalistic will on German politics and society. Boycotts of Jewish-owned businesses were called. By August 1934, Hitler would be elected fuhrer.

Julius had worked for a bank in Fürth. He realized things were getting difficult because he noticed they were letting Jewish employees go. He got a visa and left for Paris. So that was my destination.

My mother knew Mr. Laval at the French embassy in Munich. When she went to visit with him, he told her that no more visas were being issued to France. That was quite a blow.

Cecile and Julius in love, 1933

The only alternative was England. At the time, a person could go there and upon arrival, on the spot, immigration officials would decide whether to let the person in or not. If rejected, you had to make your way back. To be allowed to stay, a person must not be a burden to the state or seek employment, among other criteria. Many were sent back.

In 1935 (the exact same year that Diane was born in the far-off land of Egypt), I went to England by boat, third class.

At the immigration desk, I was fortunate enough to be let in. It was so difficult to watch as the person ahead of me was rejected! I was wearing a fur coat and fur hat, which Uncle Bert's wife had sent me from America. The fact that I was let in, I attribute to my aunt's finery: it must have made me look prosperous. As the saying goes, and particularly in that case, "clothing makes the woman." I am most grateful to my aunt who sent me lovely clothes and to the relatives who later sponsored me and helped me come to the United States, which gave me a new lease on life.

Before I left Germany, my mother had contacted two friends she had in England. One of them said I could not stay there. The other one said I could come, as they had a boardinghouse run by the Acudiste movement, a very observant Jewish Orthodox society. This boardinghouse was in London. I had to pay my way. It was forbidden to take or send money to England from Germany. Nevertheless, I was able to stay there for a few months, with help from my mother's family.

Cecile's uncle and aunt, Bert and Hilde Lehman, and family

While I was in London, Uncle Bert generously helped me financially, paying for my living expenses and education. I owe so much to him. I survived on the money he sent me on a monthly basis, as I had agreed not to work while in England. I now realize how difficult it must have been for him to take on this responsibility, as he had a wife and three children to look after while he provided for me. I was very frugal and managed to save some of this allowance, so I would have some money to go to Paris to be with Julius.

While living in London, I took exams to be admitted to a polytechnic institute. I attended classes in English and the social sciences. This education would give me teaching skills, but general knowledge was also very important to me. When I graduated, I received a certificate that allowed me to teach English in non-English-speaking countries.

After a few months, I moved to Mrs. Trout's boardinghouse. There were boarders from many different countries. While there, I witnessed the ravages of malaria. A young man had frequent attacks from the disease. That was a shock to me, as I apparently had been quite sheltered from such things. I considered Mrs. Trout's to be a transition for me, a temporary residence.

While I was there, my mother came to visit. I received her telegram minutes before her train was to pull into Victoria Station! I dashed in a cab to pick her up and reached the station just as her train was pulling in.

Unfortunately, she returned to Germany following the visit. She was still optimistic and attached to her homeland at that point.

After seven months in England, I thought it was time to try to join Julius in France. We wanted to get married. I went to the French embassy to request a visa. I was immediately turned down by a secretary.

And now, one of the most interesting events of my life took place. As I departed from the embassy, despondently and slowly, I heard footsteps behind me. A dapper gentleman wearing a bowler hat came down the steps. He asked if I would join him for a cup of tea. I immediately accepted. We went to a small tearoom and I remember that we sat outside. He ordered tea and, when he inquired, I told him my story.

It turned out that he was the French ambassador to England. After tea, he invited me to return upstairs to the Embassy. He issued me a visa to France on the spot.

I believe his name was Baron Charles Corbin. As far as I am concerned, he belongs on the list of the Righteous Ones, a designation given to the people who resisted the Nazis, or helped to hide or defend the Jews from persecution. In many cases they aided me and my family.

At last, I could finally go to Paris and be with my beloved fiancé.

That was 1936.

3

Winds of Change / Diane

Heliopolis (upper right) was a suburb of Cairo. Map: Cairo and Environs, Survey of Egypt, 1925. Source: Library of Congress

If I could pack all of the stories of our Heliopolis childhood into a single volume, I am sure I could not lift it. Even so, I would not consider story-keeping a burden. Some may tire of hearing me reminisce, but I wish I could remember *more*. Each retelling allows me to revisit an innocence snatched from us so early in our lives.

We lived at 32 Rue Ibrahim Pasha in Heliopolis (Masr Al Gedid), the ancient city of the sun. Almost nothing remains of that suburb, northeast of Cairo. Modern Heliopolis was created in the 1920s by Baron Edouard Empain, a wealthy Belgian industrialist. This posh suburb of Cairo was built in a quaint, somewhat Moorish, style with whitewashed arcades and elegant balconies above. The recessed stores located beneath benefited from the shade provided by the arcades. This suburb was eventually swallowed up by the expansion of Cairo. Nevertheless, the area maintains its unique character. To this day, many important and wealthy people reside there, drawn by the wide avenues and the special cachet it provides. I understand that many of the old buildings that were in disrepair have recently been renovated.

When I lived in Heliopolis, it was close to the end of the tramway line from Cairo. The spot where the tram turned around was a bustling place, right in front of a beautiful movie house, the Roxy, which is still in existence and under the same name. There were always people getting on and off and young kids running behind the tram as it slowly turned around before leaving and gaining speed. The cars were always crowded with people, with some hanging from the handles.

The Sporting Club

We belonged to the Sporting Club, which had a swimming pool, tennis courts, a bowling green, beautiful flower beds, and a lovely terrace where food and drinks were served.

Originally, the club was designated for British members only. Eventually, other people were allowed to join, such as the intellectual elite. And that is when my family joined. At that time, the native population was not allowed to join. Now, the members are all local.

Because of the hot weather, we went to the club to swim almost every day. At some point, my parents bought beautiful British Raleigh bikes for my older sister and me. We were so proud of them, and they allowed us to go off on our own to the club as we were a little older.

At the Sporting Club in Heliopolis, beautiful flower beds were meticulously maintained by the gardeners. This is probably where I got my passion for everything floral. I often chatted with the gardeners, who were very proud of their work, and rightly so. The flower beds were very cleverly designed with the tallest flowers in the back, while the colors were skillfully selected to harmonize. Soil from the Nile was used to enrich the beds, which were watered regularly. The displays were spectacular and the powerful scent of the flowers was intoxicating, particularly the tuberoses. The bowling green with the closely clipped grass was really green and wonderful to walk on, and it was the place where the British ladies played croquet. All this was in contrast to the sand all around.

A few years ago, I visited a farmer's market, walked by a flower stand and came to a complete stop. I had been drawn by the scent of tuberoses. It had been a while but the memory had lingered on. I immediately purchased a dozen and became friendly with the grower. I still do that every chance I get. I guess that is why I am partial to the perfumes based on jasmine (which grew on our balcony in Egypt) and tuberoses, which my mother often purchased for our home. I also have memories of the light breezes carrying the perfume of jasmine, bougainvillea, and roses in the warm Egyptian evening air.

And how about the tennis court with its pounded-smooth surface! Young kids—our age—were at our disposal to retrieve the balls. These children who had never known school ran around barefoot in uniform to serve us. When questioned about this situation, my father, who always taught us to respect working people, said that the boys were working to help their families. In addition to the pay they earned from the club, the players tipped them.

It was at the Sporting Club that I learned how to swim in the large pool—more than thirty meters long and with high diving boards. My sister Gisele was an excellent high diver! She once fell off the diving board, but was not too badly hurt.

Tables and umbrellas were laid out around the pool and the balconies above, in the shade, where we were served delicious afternoon collations after the swimming had given us an appetite. During WWII, British officers and their families were part of the scenery. My father became friendly with one of the officers. One year, he ordered Winnie-the-Pooh books for us from England and inscribed them to us as a gift. My daughter still has this heirloom.

Street Vendors and Open Markets

The streets of Cairo were crowded, dirty, and very busy; noisy and full of life and activity. People talked loudly and gesticulated while deafening noise came from the honking horns of all the foreign cars fighting for space in the totally unregulated traffic.

Flies were everywhere, but not ignored. People used horsehair whisks to nonchalantly shoo them away, as well as fly swatters which were very commonly used to squash flies, ants, and mosquitoes, sometimes right there on the tables with no one complaining! Strips of fly paper were everywhere and sometimes Flite was used to clear the air (Flite is a liquid repellant that is pushed into the air by a hand-operated pump.)

At this time in Egypt, refrigerators were quite rare. They were imported and their motors frequently broke down because the local electricity was unreliable. In my home, we had an ice box in the hallway. Ice was delivered daily because it melted so quickly in the heat. Foodstuffs were purchased daily in permanent open markets or from ambulatory vendors.

One unusual place we occasionally went to shop was the Khan El-Khalili, the well-known Cairo open-air market. There were huge mounds of various herbs and spices with all their intoxicating scents intermixing. In addition to food and related products, jewelry, traditional metal work, and souvenirs were sold. Even today, tourists flock to this historic market.

In fascination, I watched the makers of thread dough for the *konafa*, a Middle Eastern pastry dessert. A large metal surface was placed over a hot fire. The dough was poured into metal pitchers with holes in the bottom. They would skillfully run the pitchers with the holes around the wide flat cooking surface and almost immediately gather the threads with their bare hands as they cooked very fast. The bundles of dough were then rolled up with pistachios or other nuts and sometimes covered with *eichta*, a popular cream, to create the beloved dessert.

We drank water which was stored in *gargoulettes*. They are clay pots with very narrow necks which keep the water cool as they sweat. These were placed in the corner of the kitchen, which was equipped with a gas stove, quite unusual at the time.

Every spring, the khamsin arrived. It is a hot desert wind which blows for about forty to fifty days between May and June. It is incessant, pervasive, and covers everything with a fine coat of sand. Everything we tried to keep the sand out was useless. That is where the *gargoulettes* came in handy, as the sand could not get into the cool water stored there.

As I was growing up, the street vendors and performers were a major part of the scene on the street below our balcony. Performing monkeys were quite popular with the kids. Sometimes, to our delight, other performers would appear. As we lived on the third floor, the entertainers were paid by coins thrown down from the balconies, and they had to scramble for them as they bounced off the street; or the money was delivered by small baskets attached to a string and lowered down. Sometimes we made small packets and threw the money down.

Talk about diversity! The conversations across the balconies and the verandas were quite intense as we all talked to each other and had friends everywhere. It was quite a babble of languages. The communities included descendants of the Christian Copts, who had lived in Egypt since the time of the pharaohs; Greek Orthodox; Armenians; Turk descendants of the Ottoman Empire who were actually the titular powerhouse of the country; Syrians; Moslems; Lebanese, Sudanese, and Berbers. A few British and French were also scattered here and there. There was a comfortable blending of cultures: for example, my mother was a good belly dancer!

The Jews had their specific quarter, La Harte El Yahoud in the business district close to the Khan El-Khalili Bazar, but blended in with all the other sects in the population. The religious holidays of every faith were respected by one and all.

At that time, Egypt was the cultural center of Arab Muslim culture, with its educated population and many school teachers dispersed all over the Arab-speaking world. Movies, musical comedies, romances or dramas were very popular, including the actors from beyond Egypt's borders.

Entertaining and Social Life

In the old days, while killing time late in the afternoon in the noisy cafes, men (mostly) munched on salted black watermelon seeds or white seeds from other melons, and they spit out the skins on the ground. Pistachios as well as peanuts were laid out. Green and black olives were served with feta cheese, sometimes with a variety of marinated vegetables. For men, these snacks were served with Arak (an alcoholic white wine drink which contains anise), Stella beer, Coca-Cola, tea, or coffee, while they played games such as dominos and backgammon. They also smoked their hookahs and worried with their beautiful worry beads!

Women participated in some of these activities at home, mostly playing cards and munching on delicacies prepared by the hostess and her staff. All this food made them thirsty, so lemonade, Coca-Cola, and Turkish coffee were served. When they finished drinking the strong Turkish coffee, the cup was turned upside down in the saucer and they waited as the coffee grinds dripped down the sides onto the saucer. Women who were in the know, would read your fortune from the grinds left in the cup.

Our parents would frequently take us, all dressed up, to Groppi, a pastry shop in Cairo and later in Heliopolis, when they opened a closer location. At those famous bakeries, we ate ice creams, European pastries such as chocolate éclairs and mille-feuilles. At some point, Mansoura, another specialty bakery, also opened in Heliopolis. That store later opened in Brooklyn, New York, to the delight of the Egyptian diaspora as well as all lovers of quality Middle Eastern specialties, pastries, chocolates, and various confections. During my visit back to Egypt in 1985, I took my husband and daughter to Groppi. It was a shell of what it used to be. It was difficult to describe it to them, what it was like in the past, but . . . it is still around.

As kids, we felt very special when my uncle would invite us to have English high tea or Turkish coffee accompanied with pastries at the luxurious Mena House, a posh hotel where he worked in Cairo, or at the one close to the pyramids.

Savory Memories: The Foods of Egypt

With the history of my family dating back to Aleppo in Syria, it is no wonder that all my family were and still are excellent cooks.

Cairo has traditionally been known as a center for excellent cuisine since the time of the pharaohs. We prepared foods of many traditions and also creatively incorporated ideas and products from many different cultures.

I particularly remember the food staples and delicacies of my childhood, and feel that it is at a young age that one develops likes and dislikes. The climate and rich soil of Egypt are conducive to growing a great variety of quality fruits and vegetables.

Doah

Doah (pronounced DO-AH) is a traditional Egyptian seasoned dip to serve with bread. It's easy to prepare and, for me, a taste of home. Here is my recipe:

Two measures of sesame seeds
One measure of coriander seeds
Small amount of ground cumin
Salt and pepper
Frying pan
Bread (flatbread or pita)
Olive oil

Over a low heat, warm a frying pan (no oil) and add the sesame, coriander, and cumin until the spices are lightly toasted. It will only take a few minutes. Add a sprinkle of salt and pepper to taste. Don't overcook. Transfer the toasted flavorings to a clean meat grinder, spice grinder, or blender. (The blender works but is not as satisfactory as the texture comes out different.)

To serve: pour a small amount of good olive oil into a dish or bowl. Dip bread into the olive oil then into the prepared *doah*.

We enjoyed dishes from Greece, France, and all across the Middle East. Italian food was also popular. We had, among other things:

From Greece: delicious *loucoumades*, deep-fried puff pastry served with very sweet syrup and sprinkled with cinnamon.

From the Middle East: most famous of all is falafel and pita bread, now well known the world over. The original version of the pita bread pocket, which is considered a peasant bread, is much heavier and tastier when warm. The current version sold in American markets is thinner and lighter to accommodate more modern and broader tastes. The flat pocket bread is filled with falafels, that is, round fried balls (or flat ones) made from fava beans or chickpeas with spices added. Everyone adds their favorite toppings and it varies from country to country. To make it authentic, *tahina* is a must, then chopped tomatoes, cucumbers, marinated cabbage, etc., are added. It is sold as a street food in many countries.

For dessert we had a choice: *menenas*, a pie-type of dough stuffed with dates or nuts; or *konafas* (the thread-like dough mentioned previously). Baklava was filled with almonds, walnuts or pistachios, baked and then basted with syrup flavored with rose water.

I remember the singsong call of the strolling vendors of fresh sugar cane. The vendors peeled the pieces of the outer skin revealing the somewhat tender parts of the sugar cane. We munched on them with delight as the juice trickled down our chins.

Then there was the vendor selling licorice juice, as he carried his glass container on a leather strap wound around his chest, and poured the drink from a spigot.

In those days, the milk was fresh, neither treated nor pasteurized. It was sold by the milkman who made his rounds with a cart drawn by a donkey. With a wide scoop he measured out the milk into our pails. It was delicious and gave a great profusion of heavy sweet cream which was served with the desserts. Sometimes a goat accompanied the vendor, to be milked on the spot.

How about *amardeen* (dried apricot paste), which we fashioned into cones? We placed an ice cube inside and then greedily sucked on the flavored juice from the bottom tip.

Here are some additional tastes of home:

Lupin beans: prepared by soaking them in salted water. They become soft enough to gently squeeze the bean from the skin and pop into your mouth.

Turnips: cut up and placed in salty water with a couple pieces of beet to color them a beautiful pink.

Bracelets: this is what *we* called a particular baked treat because, after you buy them, you can carry them on your wrist. It is made of delicious bread dough sprinkled with sesame seeds, and they can now be found on the streets of several other countries.

Sambousek is also a delight. It is pie dough stuffed with cheeses, or cheeses and spinach. All of my family members have learned to make savory cheese triangles with filo dough. Family and guests expect them at every gathering. Thin strips of the dough are made up into small triangles stuffed with a cheese or mixed cheeses, spinach, chicken, and so on. This is the ubiquitous dough that comes in very fine sheets, used to make the exquisite baklava. These sheets must be handled with great care as they are brittle and dry out quickly. The flat sheets are rolled up and sold in boxes. When working with the dough, it is important to gently wrap it in a towel. Here is the sequence: you open the towel, roll out the dough and pull out the number of sheets you want and roll the towel back up. You do what you want with those sheets, place them on a tray and move on to the next.

The Egyptian climate and soil provided us with luscious tomatoes and flavorful pickling cucumbers, *always sprinkled with salt* to bring out the delicate flavor. They are frequently included in yogurt. I recall the eggplants which had been charred and delicately sautéed in oil, stuffed squash, and grape leaves.

I cannot leave out *ful medames*, a dish with a very old tradition. It is the national Egyptian dish, which consists of broad brown fava beans cooked with garlic. They are served up warm, swimming in their juices with olive oil, lemon juice, and *hamine* (hard-boiled eggs). The eggs are cooked for several hours with onion skins so they become brown and delicious. The yellows are then quite soft.

We enjoyed lush yellow melons, watermelons, and a wide variety of fresh dates—yellow, black, and brown; stringless mangoes; figs of different colors and tastes; apricots; and grapes. Fruit from the citrus family were also delicious:

oranges, tangerines heavy with juice, bitter and sweet lemons. The skin of the oranges was used to prepare traditional British marmalade.

Ominous Rumblings

How can I describe in just a few pages how comfortable we felt in our reality of safe childhood, even as the world around us changed?

All was not sweet in 1947-1948, though my young siblings and I were largely sheltered from the adult world of geopolitics and the rumblings in Egypt foreshadowing the civil war. We had been raised to expect tolerance in cosmo-politan and multicultural Cairo and its suburbs. As children, we had known only a live-and-let-live attitude among our middle-class Arab, Copt, Italian, Greek, and Jewish neighbors, as well as the community's merchants and the household help. So, when the rumors of conflict began, we were not prepared for upheaval. We know now that an undercurrent of nationalism was erupting into a chaotic movement. Our parents' affiliation with British and European culture would no longer protect our status. Eventually, antisemitism also boiled over in public dis-plays of hatred.

Though we did not ourselves witness or experience acts of violence, except for my sister Gisele who had a close call, rumors began to circulate in our com-munity, describing attacks on Jews, particularly Jewish girls. By 1948, even the children understood the increasing dangers in the streets of Heliopolis. Forces we could neither see nor comprehend frightened our parents so much that they grew willing to risk everything, to abandon their modest wealth and to flee ahead of societal breakdowns they believed were sure to come.

To put our dilemma in context, it helps to understand a bit of Egypt's colonial and modern history. Egypt was made a British protectorate in 1914. However, many of the people and politicians chafed at the imposition of outside rule, and years of unrest followed. In 1922, Britain signed a treaty of alliance giving Egypt its independence as a kingdom, but maintained military control in the Suez Canal zone and dominated many aspects of government. By the time my family was living in Heliopolis, society was stratified and multiethnic, and Britain continued to assert itself.

Resisting this vestige of colonialism, Egypt's king continued to press for the British to leave; in 1936, a treaty called for the British to depart by 1949. During WWII, Britain found itself defending its interests as Fascist Italian forces and then the Germans invaded and had to be repulsed before they reached Cairo. Egypt became a base for Allied operations in the region, but anti-British sentiment continued to grow, now with overseas agitators including the Nazis hoping to undermine Britain.

Meanwhile, in an attempt to resolve Middle East regional conflicts, the United Nations decided in 1947 to divide nearby Palestine into an Arab state and a Jewish state. The first Arab-Israeli War began in May 1948 after Israeli statehood was declared. Neighboring Arab nations, including Egypt, each harboring desires to control the land, sided with the Palestinians and launched attacks. Throughout the war, the bloodshed in Palestine continued. Adults shared reports in the news with each other, not with us children.

In 1948, there was great jubilation in my circles at the establishment of the State of Israel. I am delighted that Hebrew, the poetic spiritual connection of the Jewish people, became a living spoken language, in addition to a religious one, during my lifetime in Israel. The emphasis on Sephardic pronunciation was a delight, as that was what I grew up with.

The Keren Kayemet box (see image), the little blue box from the Jewish National Fund, was always in our home. We were encouraged to add coins so that the State of Israel could buy land. Two million acres were purchased with money collected worldwide for many years through this program, which continues to this day. The money is now mostly invested in water projects, reforestation, and conservation. The box is no longer blue and is now reusable. The Jewish National Fund is the largest private landowner in the State of Israel. It has been purchasing the land with money collected from these boxes

Jewish National Fund savings box

for a very long time. The fund holds one third of the landmass of the country. One half is primarily residential from which it derives income. The other half is forests and parks. It negotiated several land swaps with other countries such as Jordan as political shifts took place.

For our family, the beginning of the end in Egypt arrived with the shocking news of random attacks on our neighborhood's streets. Young Arab men were harassing and assaulting Jewish girls in broad daylight, we were told. Why? We didn't know then and we don't really know today. We can surmise that they felt emboldened at a time of fraying tolerance in what must have been a stewpot of anti-British sentiment, Arab nationalism, and antagonism spurred by the ongoing war with Israel.

As the weeks passed, the assaults escalated to shootings. My parents confirmed what was whispered in the streets: we were at risk. Then, by word of mouth, the news arrived that a girl in our community was shot at and wounded while riding her bike in broad daylight. We all heard this from the other families in the neighborhood. The attacks were directed at Jewish girls only, not boys. Gisele was accosted while walking on the street with her non-Jewish Greek friend. She was saved by her friend, who boldly confronted the hooligans and threatened them. They retreated.

My parents pulled us out of our schools. We were ordered to stay in the apartment. We were not permitted to attend ballet or youth group, to go to the sporting club or the swimming pool. We could not ride our bicycles.

The escalation of violence toward girls achieved its evil intent. With three daughters to protect while he was frequently out of the country tending to his import-export business, my father agonized. My mother, with fear and tears in her eyes, told us that the family would have to move. We must leave Heliopolis. We must leave Egypt. My parents could foresee the terrible things to come in the menacing rumblings around us.

As we broke the news to friends and family members, many could not understand why we were leaving in such haste, but my parents trusted their instincts and their knowledge of history. They believed that in the brewing turmoil, harsh treatment lay ahead for the Jews of Egypt. Many of our relatives refused to go: they felt that the intimidation would not get worse. Others could not envision their comfortable lives changing because Egypt had always been home. Some stayed rather than sacrifice investments they were sure to lose if they left the country. But my parents had made their choice: we would leave— without wealth, but with our dignity intact. And, as we now say, we left with our lives.

Our father departed again for Europe. I thought he was traveling on business as usual. My older brother set the record straight for me many years later: our father was searching for a way to get us out and a place to resettle. As children, we had only an inkling of the bureaucratic hurdles that would entail.

Our father had an Italian passport, which he used to travel for work. My mother would need one, for herself and all of us children, too.

In those days, and in that part of the world, citizenship was not determined by a person's place of birth. A woman's citizenship would depend on her father's.

It was also the custom that a woman assumed the citizenship of her husband after she married.

Maman's father was born in Jerusalem, and later immigrated to Algeria to find employment. While there, he obtained French citizenship. My mother, born later in Egypt, would be considered a French citizen as well.

Though he was born in Egypt, my father's passport was Italian. His grandfather came from the city of Livorno, Italy, so he carried Italian citizenship. That granted Italian citizenship to his son, and later, my father, though he, too, was born in Egypt. That made us Italian, too.

Italian passport of Esther Yedid and her children. Diane is standing at center.

Our Italian passports are heirlooms. Eventually each of us had a personal passport, but for our departure from Egypt, the Italian Embassy in Cairo issued a group passport. It is dated October 8, 1947, and affixed inside is a portrait of my mother and all five children.

In the faces, I see glimmers of my siblings' personalities and my mother's resolve. Maman sits at the center, maybe a little tired, smiling faintly. I am standing behind her, and today, I am surprised to see myself wearing my hair long, as I was tender-headed and found combing painful. My gaze looks dazed or slightly shell-shocked. I always say that I handled that strained time of change in our lives like I was walking in a fog. I am wearing a Star of David pendant given to me as a gift by a relative who had visited Palestine.

Gisele, the eldest child, is to my mother's right, and Joyce is down front: both look vivacious and excited. All the girls, like Maman, wear floral or printed dresses with ruffles at the bodice popular at the time.

Alain, the older boy, looks studious. Danny, our youngest, looks sleepy-eyed. The boys stand together to Maman's left, wearing crisp white shirts with short sleeves.

I do not recall posing for the picture. I do not recognize the background. I only know that once we had that passport, Egypt was no longer our home.

As I write this, I am aware that some readers will consider it controversial that I use the word "home" in connection with Egypt. Nostalgia may seem as natural as breathing to others, but it is not for many of the Jewish refugees of Egypt from my generation—those who departed around the time of the Arab-Israeli War in 1948 right up through those expelled from Egypt in 1956.

Thousands of us assimilated to the customs and languages of our various destinations. Many were taught by their parents to erase rather than cherish any ties to Egypt. Others believed that resurrecting the old stories would be akin to complaining. After all, we survived, didn't we? Look at the Holocaust victims who suffered more. Our lives weren't so bad.

Since then, several nonprofit, academic, and cultural organizations devoted to preserving the diaspora stories of Egyptian Jews have emerged. These forums, aided by the internet, encourage us to publicly share the tales we might have previously revealed only among ourselves. Before there is no one left who remembers, we are called to chronicle our stories.

In fact, as children, our parents told us, "Forget Egypt. Do not look back. Turn your face toward a better future." Is it any wonder that some who grew up in Heliopolis cannot look back? Others are compelled to stare down the timeline of history and claim their place on it, no matter what misgivings or discomforts they feel.

I was obedient when my parents told us not to dwell on the past. Today, however, I choose not to deny these essential chapters in the story of the child I was and the woman I have become. Where would I be had I not tasted the milk and honey of a secure and happy childhood, as well as the bitter herbs of our exodus from the only place we knew as home? Heritage and identity should trump politics, but this is the refugee's burden: with the unknown on the horizon, and threats at our heels, how do we embrace our roots?

Flight from Egypt

At age fourteen, I faced the news that we were going away with equal parts of excitement and trepidation. In exile already in the apartment, I was lucky to have so many siblings to play with. There were not many other children in our building. I missed our friends and I missed school and our other activities. Meanwhile, everything I knew to be cemented was coming unglued.

With my father away in Europe, the closing of the apartment and his office, and the selling off or giving away of all our possessions, fell to my mother, a woman on her own, in a Middle Eastern country in 1948 with five children. She accomplished this feat with the help and support of the family.

My mother decreed what was important for us to take: the sewing machine, the bicycles (who could imagine leaving our Raleigh bikes behind?), the photo albums, some linens. Our belongings would be reduced to what could fit into two crates and a few suitcases packed by the weeping servant women.

One of the important memories of my school days, which I chose to include in the very few things we had the possibility of taking with us, was the autograph book I'd had since 1947. It was very common for all my friends to have one. Mine is bound in blue suede and includes many friendship messages and poems from long-ago friends. Some messages have exquisite colorful drawings or whimsical quotes. These books usually contained what we called "The Wall of Friendship," which had boxes outlined for your friends to sign. Mine is empty, because of our hasty departure! I treasure the autograph book as a fond memory of my school days gone by. Of course, I have lost touch with all those people.

Restrictions on carrying Egyptian currency out of the country meant that my mother needed to spend what we could not take. After that, we would give away or forfeit the rest of the family's cash. From notations and stamps inside the passport, we know that our family received permission to carry only seventy-five pounds British sterling as we left Egypt on our "return" to Italy. (In US dollars, in 1948, that would have been roughly three hundred; in today's dollars, to put this in context, the equivalent would be about 3,400 dollars. Not much to launch a family with five children in a new land. Unless my father had managed to spirit other funds out when he left, that was all we would have to start our new life.)

There was another way of spiriting assets out of Egypt. All women in that culture wore gold bracelets. It was very traditional. As we were leaving, we were instructed to make sure that our bracelets were tucked inside our clothes and not visible. Eventually, when things got very rough, all the bracelets were sold, one by one, to help keep us afloat. It really bothered my parents that we would not have any gold bracelets! A few years later, when my parents' financial situation got better, they went on a holiday to Majorca on the coast of Spain. When they came back, my father handed me three beautiful gold embossed bracelets and said to me, "Here are your bracelets!" It was a very touching moment. I still have and wear them.

As a way of spending down some of our family's money, Maman brought in the sewing lady. Regardless of the season, well-made clothes were expensive and not readily available off-the-rack in Egypt in the 1940s. We had a regular seamstress, who arrived at the change of seasons to mend and update or create garments for our growing family. Her work would go on for days at a stretch—there were six of us! During this final visit, her assignment was to prepare us for our first freezing winter in Italy. She sewed jumpers and long-sleeved shirts and coats. How we hated the itchy woolens, unfamiliar fabric for children of the Middle Eastern climate. When she left for the last time, I remember, profuse tears were shed.

As the weeks passed, I noticed people coming and going from our apartment, snickering at the prices my mother asked as she attempted to sell off possessions. They knew she could not take these items with us. Many waited until she was desperate and the prices were as low as they could expect. She gave away many things and abandoned many more. We understood she did well when she sold our telephone. They were at the time relatively hard to come by in Egypt: a telephone was a symbol of wealth and contacts. As soon as the word was out that my mother had a telephone for sale, an army officer came to the door and told her he wanted to buy it. He was very respectful and pleasant. They concluded on a fair price and he paid her on the spot. He offered to allow her to keep it until she would be leaving, and he would send someone over to pick it up. On the appointed day, he showed up himself, thanked my mother and wished her good luck. My mother always said he had been quite a gentleman.

Stranded indoors, I also eavesdropped on my mother's emotional farewells as she let go the household staff. I remember the wailing of the maids, who insisted that no one would treat them as well as my family had. Most came from rural families. In our apartment, they learned skills from my mother, and had a decent place to sleep, meals, and a wage. Some feared they would end up working in homes less humane, where they might be beaten; others worried about returning to their villages and lives of poverty. Also, I saw anguish in the eyes of the doorman's wife as she spoke with my mother. She was losing a friend who cared about her fate.

When the time came to leave, we departed for Alexandria, two days travel from Cairo. My mother's sister Victorine and her husband Benoit, and other relatives, joined us at the port.

The day of our escape is still fresh in my mind's eye as if it had happened yesterday.

At the appointed hour, we huddled with these relatives and our two small crates and few suitcases by the gangplank of the *Filippo Grimani*, a steamship of the Adriatica Line that would take us away from Egypt across the Mediterranean Sea to Europe, to Genoa. The horn sounded, as well as shouts of "All aboard!" It looked like a seaworthy vessel, with planks lowered to facilitate our climbing to the ship. With proper documents and Italian passport in hand, it looked like an easy way to flee.

Then, an official wearing a red fez stepped forward, barring our way.

"The water bill is unpaid," he proclaimed, examining our papers. "You must return to Cairo, pay, and get a receipt," he said.

This was a common ploy to harass and secure bribes. Protesting, my mother presented the proof of the payment for the municipal water service. The official airily waved it aside.

The relatives conferred, and then offered to pay the account again, to no avail. Arguing that we had no time, no house to return to, and no money, also proved fruitless.

My mother cried. My siblings and I screamed and wailed. The relatives stood by helplessly while the officer preened.

The ship's horn sounded again and again.

The captain appeared at the dock. He tried to persuade the official to let us board the ship, and then regretfully warned my mother that we would be left behind if the trouble was not resolved very rapidly.

Pandemonium broke out. Then my uncle Benoit, a smart man of the world, pulled the official aside. We witnessed the whispers and the bobbing of the heads, the gesticulating and nodding. Uncle Benoit prevailed, sealing an agreement with a very fat handshake (meaning a bribe).

Debts waived, crates lifted. We grabbed our suitcases and sprinted up the gangplank.

4

Winds of Change / Cecile

Cecile and Julius Wasserman, newlyweds in Paris, 1937

When Julius arrived in Paris, he could barely speak French. He could not find a job. An older cousin, also named Julius Wasserman, worked as a salesman in the zipper business—*fermeture éclair.* This was a relatively new product made in Czechoslovakia. His cousin got my Julius to work with him.

After a while, the prefecture told Julius he could not stay or work because he did not have legal status. In desperation, he went to Belgium for a short stay. While Julius was there, he was able to obtain a visa to France so he was legal for a while and able to work with his cousin, mostly in Paris.

Once I met up with Julius in Paris, it took several months for us to make the necessary arrangements for our wedding. We were married in January 1937 by the justice of the peace at the Mairie du 10eme Arrondisement, Avenue Victor Hugo. Two friends were the witnesses and I wore the only dress I owned. My mother was very distressed that there were no family members present at the wedding of her only child. I also felt very sad about that.

As far as our honeymoon is concerned, it was quite an unusual event. Nothing was easy in those times. Julius was going on a business trip to Belgium, then on to London. I had to travel alone from Paris to Bruxelles, where we met. In Belgium, we visited Antwerp. I immediately liked the city because of the architecture.

We then returned to Bruxelles. When we hopped into a cab, the driver immediately took a liking to us. He was Flemish and spoke French beautifully. He took us around the city all day. We were again very impressed by the architectural style of that city. Best of all, we ended up at his wife's tea salon for tea and cookies. It was so heartwarming to connect on a personal level.

On to London, where Julius had to conduct some business. The rest of the time we devoted to each other and having a good time using the scarce resources we had left.

Julius and I had a relationship based on strong principles and were very devoted to each other. It was with great dismay that we watched many young people who had left their families behind, having no more parental and societal pressures, yield to the many temptations of Paris in that era. Several lives were affected and many permanently damaged or destroyed.

In Paris, we first lived in an empty apartment on Rue d'Hauteville, which also contained the office. It was drab without any amenities. It had only one bed and a small kitchen. As we had no refrigeration, I shopped every other day at the open markets in the streets of Paris buying fruit and vegetables. Although I was not a very good cook, I used a notebook where I had written my aunt Regina's recipes, and managed to prepare meals for six people every day, which included Julius and I, his associate Mr. Hammer and his wife, as well as Mr. Hammer's cousin and her brother.

I had a great time walking the streets of Paris at that time. I would make up stories in my head about the people I saw on the street such as where they came from and what their lives were like. I did the same on the Métro and would sometimes miss my stop . . .

At some point, I got very sick with paratyphoid from eating ice cream from a street vendor. I landed in the hospital for two weeks and could not eat for three weeks. Then I could only take soup. I am a slight person so during that time, when I lost thirty pounds, I became quite thin. After that episode I could only eat vegetables for several months. I frequented the market on Ave St. Denis where I would obtain very fresh vegetables from the farmers. I remember that the doctor attributed my illness to living under difficult conditions with no furniture in sight. I thought it was ridiculous! This was just the way things were and I took it all in stride.

During that time, for approximately one year, I was very careful not to say a word in French around my husband's associates, as I was concerned about my mastery of the French language. The only basis of my skill for speaking the language was the French I took in school when I was young. So I took French lessons to improve my knowledge and speaking abilities. I managed to do my own shopping and made my way around quite well.

Precious Time with Family

At some point, Julius's parents came from Germany to visit. We were delighted to see them. Although we had scarce resources (to my husband's dismay), it was my pleasure to purchase a very special outfit for my mother-in-law. It was a lovely black suit with a matching black hat. She was a large, statuesque woman and she looked stunning in the outfit. That made me very happy.

During their stay, I remember that every day we went to a restaurant called Tout vas Bien (Everything is OK), where we could have a good meal for the reasonable cost of eight francs per person. That was a lot of money anyway because, after all, we were four. I recall that we went to the movies and saw Charlie Chaplin in *Modern Times.*

Later, to my joy, my mother also came to visit. Unfortunately, at that time I came down with appendicitis and she had to leave before the operation. I still found the strength to take her to the train station, along with Julius. It was a very moving moment when, as the train was pulling away, she stretched out her arms and blessed us. We all had dark premonitions. Change was in the air! I could sense it.

To recuperate after my surgery, as was the custom at the time, Julius sent me to Le Tregas, in the Alpes-Maritimes. The air was good and I spent one month there. I had a chance to make friends with several people. That was a trait I'd always had and continue to have.

While I was there, I met a French woman with a fourteen-year-old son. We became friends. (They later came to visit us while we lived in Epinay. We exchanged visits a couple of times. When we eventually escaped to Eyrein, I received a very long, four-page letter—in PERFECT GERMAN!—saying we should get together, etc. I was then convinced that she was a SPY! Otherwise how could she have gotten our address?)

I saw my mother again after I recovered from the operation. I was able to meet her in St. Remo, a resort on the border of France and Italy on the Côte d'Azur. At that time, it was easier to obtain a visa for Italy than France, so we met there. We spent two weeks together. We just simply enjoyed each other in the Italian resort atmosphere. The service in the hotel was impeccable and the memory of it all is very sweet. We went to the beach every day.

One day while on the beach, a very handsome young German whom I noticed was reading a Nazi newspaper, approached me and wanted to make conversation. I told him right away that I was Jewish and that cut him off immediately! He walked away.

This trip to St. Remo was indeed the last time I saw my mother. I feel very strongly the energy that she always projected towards me. I believe that even when she was in the concentration camp and dying, she was praying for me and I believe that is where my strength comes from.

As visas and money became harder to come by, visits from family, which were few and far between, were very precious to us. My aunt Paula and uncle Ludwig Kurtzman were a very happy couple. I joyfully welcomed them to Paris when they came to visit Julius and me. I particularly remember that we went to a cabaret and my uncle was scandalized and could not believe we had taken him to such a place.

Cecile in Epinay, France, 1939

A Close Call

From Paris, we moved to a rented house in Épinay-sur-Seine, a lovely place in the beautiful French countryside. One of the pleasant walks was to Studio Éclair where movies were made. The best walk of all, though, was a path that led to Enghien-les-Bains, a resort area with an elegant casino. It was so pleasant to sit outside the casino and look at the lake.

One afternoon, I stretched a hammock in the garden and lay there thinking about the war. It was coming, I knew. It was unavoidable. I still clearly remember that I looked up at the clear blue sky and wondered how long peace would last!

While we lived in Eyrein, we read a newspaper called *Le Journal de Geneve.* It reported the world situation better than any other around. The other newspapers had to follow tight censorship.

It is amazing how things worked in those times. I once ran across some Germans in a car. It was lucky that I looked German and not Jewish. They thought I was a German spy and they were most respectful of me and let me go. Once, while in Alsace with Julius, we saw a German parade and I got bad premonitions and was truly scared.

One day, Julius and I were on the crest of a hill, in the Vosges mountains, close to Gérardmer. As we looked down over the countryside, we saw soldiers dressed in green, trying to blend into the landscape. At that moment we had more premonitions.

Once on an outing, we met a man who asked us many questions. We were very concerned and rightly so because the next day Julius was called into the prefecture where they checked his papers. The fear was palpable.

The war broke out in 1939. France started sending all the young men to the front. Julius attempted to join but foreigners, particularly from Germany, were not allowed to join the French forces because they did not know if these men could be trusted.

Instead, Julius was sent to stay and work with a farmer in Normandy. I remained in Paris. Although he was a city person, Julius adapted easily to country life. He worked on that farm doing many different jobs. He was occasionally given time off and was able to come home and visit. I was also able to visit him several times. While visiting him I was treated quite well and given a very nice bedroom during my stay.

One day while I was napping, I was startled by a click. . . . I quickly realized that my purse, which was on a chair to my right side, had been opened and my wallet taken. I somehow knew that the cook's eleven-year-old son was responsible. When I confronted the mother, she denied it vehemently. What ensued was a long diatribe against the Germans. She apparently did not realize that I was a different kind of German. I never got my money back.

Julius was eventually able to enlist in the French Foreign Legion, which was a pretty tough outfit! All the men in his category applied and got special exemptions.

They could sign up for the duration of the war, which of course was an indeterminate period of time. He looked smashing in his uniform. He came back home for a short period of time before he left for duty in Morocco. He was there during the Jewish holidays and a family actually invited him to their home for the celebration.

The Germans at some point parachuted women into Belgium, where they cut the telephone lines and disrupted all communications. So, back in France, from one day to the next, the women of German origin had to report to the Vélodrome d'Hiver in Paris, as we were also considered a risk. They told us not to bring anything because we only had to report and be there for a short period of time.

Most of us had brought no food and none was provided. Some had brought oranges and apples. We all begged them for some food as we were getting quite hungry. There were approximately four hundred of us, but there was nonetheless a nice camaraderie between us. It turned out that we spent the night there. Several women became hysterical and screamed all night. It was a terrible scene.

I was the only one pregnant in the group. The doctor examined me on the spot and sent me back home. I was relieved to be sent back and felt so lucky. I learned that all the other women were sent to a location next to the Spanish border.

Very soon afterwards, a V-2 bomb fell on Montmorency, a suburb close to Épinay-sur-Seine where I lived. I immediately decided it was unsafe to stay there. I packed a suitcase and among the things I took, I do not know why, were four of Julius's zipper sample jackets, which eventually came in very handy.

When I reached the Gare d'Austerlitz, I was greeted by a sea of humanity! Thousands of people were there.

Not knowing what to do, I sat on my suitcase until I was able to take a train to anywhere . . . The train I took, by chance, went in the direction of

Cecile, 1939

Correze in central France, and stopped in Tulle. I got off there and immediately went to the small Restaurant de la Gare and had something to eat. In the countryside, people were still able to eat well. Four courses were the standard.

Living in Hiding

Not knowing what to do, and being on my own, I had to think quickly, on my feet. I went to the maternity hospital across the street from the prefecture. Necessity guided me and I asked to speak to the directrice. She referred me to a woman called Leonie who was from Eyrein, a small village about two hours by train from Tulle, the capital of Correze. It seems to me that Leonie called someone in advance and asked if I could come. Once they said yes, I was on my way.

When I arrived there, I asked for a room to stay. Being afraid to say I was from Germany, I said I was Polish but they quickly found out where I was from. When I arrived, I met Mme Lacroix, a beautiful statuesque woman with four children, a boy and three girls. As the lady of the house, Mme Lacroix was very unusual. She was well in advance of her time: she was so open and kind, and very intelligent. Her family deferred to Mme Lacroix and highly respected her. She was like a goddess to her husband and her children, all well deserved. One of the most intelligent women I ever met.

Her husband, Mr. Lacroix absolutely adored his wife. Mr. Lacroix introduced me to his mother, who had a series of rooms upstairs. She immediately liked me and allowed me to rent a room and a kitchen. I had some money and was able to pay the rent.

Their daughter Gisele was thirteen when I was twenty-six and living in hiding in their farm in Eyrein. The farm was called La Maison du Bon Dieu, meaning the House of God. There was something very special about that place. It was far from other farms and a long walk from Eyrein and the train station.

At some point it was necessary for me to do something special for the Lacroix family. So, I had the opportunity to give Mme Lacroix those four zipper jackets, which was most appreciated.

Eventually, Julius came back from Morocco and was decommissioned from the French Foreign Legion. He joined me in the Correze. He found a job across the street at La Menuiserie, a noisy woodworking and carpentry workshop.

When it was time for me to give birth, I went to La Maternité de Tulle, a place dedicated to birthing and the care of mothers and babies. The birthing maternity ward was basically a destination for young pregnant unmarried women. I would like to record an incident which took place while I was there that I am still haunted by.

Elfrieda, a married Jewish German woman, and Henriette, a French woman, came to the Maternité to give birth at the same time as me. I imme-diately sensed that I did not trust Henriette because her actions appeared false to me. I've always had a sixth sense about people. I would not even accept the candies she proffered (a rare treat in those days!).

Elfrieda unfortunately gave birth to a stillborn child, while Henriette had a healthy boy. Henriette was a "smooth operator" and I could not under-stand how Elfrieda was taken in by her. Nevertheless, they became friends. Elfrieda asked Henriette if she and her husband could adopt Henriette's son, as the new mother was single. A deal was struck and Elfrieda left with the baby. After a while, Henriette denounced Elfrieda as being Jewish, who was then deported and disappeared. Henriette moved in with Elfrieda's husband and her son. I remember my shock when I received a birth announcement by the so-called parents . . .

I gave birth to my first cherished son, Marc Robert. It was a difficult and lengthy birth and I was quite sick afterwards from an infection and fever. I was fortunately very well cared for and we left in good health. I got to eat lentils every day and Julius brought me hard-boiled eggs (a dozen!) to supplement the lentils. That is all he was able to obtain. They fed us lentils because it is good for lactation.

As long as Julius was with me, I did not worry very much and felt safe. The Lacroix family was absolutely wonderful to us. They adored us and we were like their family. Mr. Lacroix's mother, "La Madioux" (a term of endearment), loved our children and always gave them des tourtoux, something like a crepe loaded with butter and sugar. One day I emptied the chamber pot out the window and it fell on an old lady's head. It turned out to be La Madioux! We all had a good laugh over that incident. She would spend time with me and always held Robert with great affection and tenderness. I was relatively insouciant during that time because it is in my nature. We were particularly lucky that Julius had a job.

Mme Lacroix, the younger, invited me from time to time to come with her when it was her turn to garder les vaches (watch the cows). I was delighted to go along because I loved the countryside. I can still see with my inner eye the peaceful, gorgeous landscape with the green pastures surrounded by forests.

While life continued on, I became pregnant again. The doctor insisted I go to La Maternité in Tulle early because he was afraid I might have a miscar-riage. I was under strict orders not to leave the place. You needed permission to leave. One day I just had to get out. On impulse I sneaked out, bought a pound of cherries, and ate the whole thing before I came back. Fortunately, nothing happened to me.

I was thrilled that Robert was able to come with me. If you had another child, you could also bring that child there with you so you could have peace of mind. He stayed with other children in another part of the building. He cried a lot but I felt safer with him close by. At the Maternité, I gave birth to Claude Richard. It was again a very difficult birth for me. When Robert and I came back with the new baby, we were warmly greeted and embraced by the Lacroix family. Another child to hold and nurture . . .

One day a salesman came to their house and during his visit he made disparaging remarks about the Jews. Mme Lacroix reamed him out and I could hear her clearly yelling all the way up the stairs. He retracted but even as he backed down and started to leave, she followed him and yelled at him not to never come back.

The Correze was initially in the *zone libre*, which later became part of the *zone occupée*. In other words, the escape to France from Germany only briefly provided sanctuary for anyone fleeing the Nazis' advance across Europe.

Vichy France Map, Rostislav Botev, 2008 (CC BY-SA 3.0)
https://commons.wikimedia.org/wiki/File:Vichy_France_Map.jpg

After fleeing Paris, Cecile found temporary sanctuary in a farm village in the mountainous Correze region, about one hundred miles southwest of Vichy, which became the de facto seat of government for much of France in the free zone during WWII. A little history: At the Second Armistice at Compiègne on 22 June 1940, France's territory was partitioned into a German occupation zone and a free zone. The free zone, south of the demarcation line, was administered by the French government of Marshal Philippe Pétain, based in Vichy. To the north lay the occupied zone, in which French powers were severely limited by German rule. However, from November 1942, both zones were under German military administration. Therefore, Cecile and Julius would be safe in Correze only briefly.

The woodworking shop where Julius worked was located a short distance away, across the street, and I could even see it from the house. It was near the only hotel in town, Hotel Beysac, and close to the train station so the goods could easily be shipped out. Julius was a very capable person and could do anything he put his mind to. He certainly was not trained for such work but he did it with patience. He was young and it was hard work, but IT WAS A JOB!

My job was to take care of the children and find food for the family, no easy task after our region became part of the occupied zone. The farmers had to sell their products on the black market to survive and I had to find other sources. I found a farmhouse where I could get milk, butter, and cheese. The cheese was made from *le petit lait* and was covered with worms! The farm was four kilometers away, up and down the vales. I had to take the children with me. I pushed them both together in a pram and later in a smaller carriage. It was very stressful yet I enjoyed the landscape.

I remember a funny incident involving the five cats living in the Lacroix household. I always placed the dairy products in the buffet and the meat in the bottom part. We had no way to keep the food refrigerated. In order to obtain meat, we had ration cards, and meat was usually sold once a week. The butcher was there only for a limited amount of time, as he left whenever he ran out of supplies.

One day, the five cats got into the buffet and spirited the meat away . . . Julius was furious. He threw a fork at them and tried to catch them, but they dashed down the steps and that was the end of this meat ration.

We thought we were well hidden in the Lacroix home, because very few people knew who we were. I remember that Mme Lacroix said that she felt we were very good people and well educated.

Pierre Martin was also living there. The Lacroix family were friends of his family. He had been staying with them because they felt he was safer there than in Paris. He had joined the Maquis (the French underground resistance fighting the Nazis) to escape being deported as a "volunteer" worker to Germany. He eventually married Gisele Lacroix.

One night, while I was still living there, I heard a bang on the door. When I opened it, I saw Gisele and Pierre standing there. They signaled me to come out. I crept out of the room. They had the idea that we should swear to love, fidelity, and friendship forever. We put our arms around each other and did just that.

But the anxiety became more marked as the region's young men, ages eighteen and older, became volunteer workers and were shipped to Germany. Those who did not want to go escaped into the woods and became part of Le Maquis.

One day, thirteen members of Le Maquis had a little too much to drink and attacked the Wehrmacht and Georgian troops in the Hotel Beysac down the street from us. (Originally, the Georgians were prisoners, but if they promised to fight with the Germans they were allowed to become part of the German forces.)

At some point shooting started and all the workers in that area started running past us into the woods. I did not see Julius. I was worried. I kept my wits about me. (I never panic!) Robert was at Tata's (the grandmother) in the other house and Richard was in the kitchen, which was in the front of the house. I went to where Robert was and left Richard behind. Once I knew that Robert was safe, I made the decision to leave him there. I came back only to find Richard absolutely terrified and screaming. He was not even two years old. Shots had been fired through the kitchen and I could see the bullet holes. I took Richard and we went to the barn for safety. I laid him down on the ground, but he kept yelling. The only way to quiet him down was to allow him to stand and I put my arms around him to calm him down. It worked and we were not detected. Meanwhile the Germans and the Georgians went through the Lacroix house looking for papers and money. They ripped the mattresses. Fortunately, they did not find anything about us.

It seemed that when the Germans came into town, the noise in the *menuiserie* did not allow the workers, including Julius, to hear the commotion, so they were caught by surprise and taken away.

A little later, somebody came up and gave me a letter. It was from Julius. In the letter, he said that he loved me and the children and was proud to die as a Jew. This letter was proof of his bravery as he indicated that he had no illusions about his fate. I could not keep the letter because it would have identified me.

I did not give up hope and very soon afterwards, I went to Tulle to see if I could find him. I went to the German headquarters, presented myself and said I would like to give someone a pair of shoes for my husband, as I felt he would need them. The soldier was very polite and kind to me. I spoke to him in German and asked if they would let him go. I was naïve . . . But I obtained no information. I left the shoes there as the soldier said he would give them to Julius. I feel that he was also one of the Righteous as he appeared to have sympathy for me. But he had no authority. Were it up to him, I feel he would have freed Julius.

I tried unsuccessfully a second time and that is when I realized and admitted to myself that I had lost Julius, the love of my life and the father of my children.

I met a woman who was in a similar situation. She was not Jewish but married to a Jewish man. She allowed me to spend the night with her while in Tulle. We were in the same boat. We shared a very uncomfortable bed that night. Life makes strange bedfellows.

In 1966, Cecile and Henri Spiegel (left) visited Gisele and Pierre Martin, who had helped hide Cecile from the Nazis.

Fifty-eight years later, two of the Lacroix daughters, Gisele and Marcelle, were still in touch with me by phone and by mail. The son, Gilbert, gave Marcelle some recent photographs to send me. They are of Holocaust memorials, one in their village with the name of my husband Julius Wasserman clearly visible, and one of the memorials in Paris. *L'dor v'dor!* (Hebrew for "From generation to generation!")

5

On the Run, with Children / Cecile

With every bit of courage I could muster, I went back to Eyrein. The Lacroix family were deathly afraid of having us in their house. Mme Lacroix felt the Germans had their address. At this point, I had no choice but to leave with the children. It was no longer safe for either them or us. I made the difficult choice to leave immediately. So began my long, tortuous odyssey.

In the morning, I took the children's carriage, which was large enough to hold them both, quickly threw in what belongings would fit, and we left. It was a matter of survival for us all. But where could I go? Which direction? For our safety, it was important to avoid the train station, so I had to travel on foot away from the village.

There were deep woods right on the edge of the village, which would allow me to move toward the Correze interior. That section of the countryside is hilly. Pushing the carriage with both children (I was only five feet tall!) was no mean feat.

I operated out of a sense of survival, not self-pity. Decisions were made in a matter-of-fact manner. It was the only option open to me. I had to react from instinct, think pragmatically, do whatever needed to be done.

I pushed the carriage uphill through the woods toward the small village of Vitrac. I had to be close to civilization because the children needed milk, food, and shelter. Once I arrived there, the townspeople, including the lady mayor, were very kind to us. She allowed me to spend the night in her house. Another Righteous person. But they were all very afraid and I had to leave in the morning. As I trekked through the woods, I came across an empty house and decided to spend the night there. All was peace and quiet until six in the morning. Then, a very loud and persistent banging on the door woke me up. I was scared as never before! We had been found and would be deported . . .

I opened the door and was so relieved to see Pierre Martin standing there. Through the grapevine, he had found out where we were and had come to check up on us. I was so grateful to him for that.

We stayed in the house only one day. I realized that I was a threat to everybody and could not place them in jeopardy. I went back to Eyrein for a few days, but it was not safe there either for anyone. I left the children in Eyrein and hitchhiked to Tulle. I had wrapped a turban around my head because my hair looked a fright. I was quickly picked up by two Germans in a car. I spoke to them in German and was surprised by the fact that they were very respectful of me and also seemed genuinely afraid of me. A mystery. Once in Tulle, I tried unsuccessfully, for the last time, to get in touch with Julius.

A thirteen-year-old girl, who was a friend of Gisele Lacroix, was staying with her grandmother in Tulle. I was welcomed and served the most amazing meals prepared by the grandmother, who railed against the Germans. She was very courageous (another Righteous One) to have me in her house as it was quite dangerous. I could not sleep while there and spent a couple very uncomfortable nights sharing a bed with another woman. Across the street was a hotel occupied by Moroccans and Algerians who were pro-German. There was constant shooting during the night. I never found out what was going on. It was very scary with not a moment's peace.

Having no more funds, I returned to Eyrein and decided it was time to really leave and look for a job to support the children and myself. I took the train with the children to Brive-la-Gaillarde. Taking the train was a risky business. You needed a permit and I did not have one. Of course, if accosted, one would be arrested immediately.

When we arrived in Brive-la-Gaillarde, I was directed to Mademoiselle Monteil, who was in charge of *un jardin d'enfants*, which consisted of a space devoted to childcare. One half of the facility was set aside for children coming only during the day. The other half was devoted to children without parents who were staying there permanently. After she heard my story, Mademoiselle Monteil reluctantly agreed to take my children on a permanent basis. Again, it took courage and compassion.

While visiting there I was struck by the plight of a Jewish man who would bring his two young boys to spend the day while he went to work. The reason he had to bring his children to the *garderie* was that his wife had been picked up one day while he and the children were out. It was so hard to hear the children scream as he left. Of course, the moment they realized he was far away they stopped! The routine took place again when he came to pick them up. I never found out what happened to him.

My priority at that point was to find a job. Mademoiselle Monteil knew that the Brossard family was looking for a chambermaid. By the time I arrived they had already found a charming young woman from La Franche Comte in the area of Alsace. I was nevertheless hired as a cook. (Who me, a cook? Ha! I never could cook.)

The chambermaid and I had to share a room on the top floor, under the eaves. I did not care much for that. Brive-la-Gaillard is a beautiful city, below sea level and very humid. I had sinus trouble and all night long I suffered from the effects. It is funny that I tried to pass as being from Alsace. She asked many incisive questions and quickly realized that I was not from Alsace. We nevertheless got along quite well even though she suspected something.

Mme Brossard knew the truth. Like everyone who took me in, she did so at great risk. Half the French people wanted to help and were even willing to risk their lives. They were the courageous ones. The other half were fence-sitters or plain collaborators.

As the cook, I was eager to learn the art from Mme Brossard, who was very capable and a good teacher. I remember her showing me how to prepare leg of lamb; just slit the meat and insert the garlic, she said. But I really did not learn very much as I do not like to cook. I was sort of an additional chambermaid and all-around helper. The Brossard family was very well off. They had two beautiful young daughters. One day I watched them sunbathing in the garden wearing their bikinis. I had a sudden surge of revolt. I could not believe that I was waiting on these lovely people while I had been the one waited on in the past.

Social status is a phenomenon I experienced with great intensity. Once one reached a lower status one was branded. During this time, I was experiencing a repetitive dream; I was tumbling and tumbling down and further down. I mentioned this dream to a French woman who interpreted it to mean that I was tumbling down the social ladder.

While in Brive-la-Gaillarde, I met Mme Duchenes and her husband. He was a colonel in the Maquis for many years. She was a remarkable woman in all ways. She would have sacrificed her life to help the Maquis or the refugees.

In Brive, I had to register with the German authorities, but I had false identity papers in the name of Lugaud and no *livret de famille*, an important document at that time. Mme Duchenes took me to a school where a friend of hers was working registering people. Her friend, at great risk, said she had seen my nonexistent *livret de famille* so that I could be registered.

I had to teach my children their new names and mine. I was now Cecile Lugaud and they were Richard and Robert Lugaud. We practiced and repeated Lugaud until it was drummed into their heads. They were very good about it and very cooperative. I believe that in some subliminal way they realized the gravity of the situation.

I managed to get the papers through a French Jewish man named Addess, who did this to help people although it was very dangerous. (Later, when I returned to Paris, I made it my mission to track him down and thank him. I was shocked that he gave me short shrift which really surprised me. Apparently, it was still quite dangerous for him.)

All along, I found these encounters uplifting. They gave me great faith in humankind. There were many French heroes who helped me in big and small ways. I did have some encounters with people who were not heroes, but they were few and far between. When I felt scared, down and out, it was like an obligation to keep going to honor these heroes, known and unknown.

One day I had a sudden and strong urge to go to the movies. That shows how important some sort of fun, diversion, or distraction is, even under dire circumstances. It was reckless because when you left the movies your identity papers were checked. I did not have my official identity papers, not even a *livret de famille*. I placed myself in extreme danger. What would have become of my dear children if I were picked up? I was lucky because they looked at my false identity papers and I passed.

Another scary incident took place while I was staying with the Brossard family. A German soldier patrolled the street in front of their house. One day, I was at the window and he spoke to me. We talked for a while in German. That was a dangerous thing! He came back repeatedly and he apparently liked me. After a few times, I realized how imprudent that was. One day, I told him I realized that he liked me but that it would be best for both of us if he stopped coming. I was fortunate that he understood and never came back. Saved again.

I am intrigued by the power of speaking your native language as that urge twice almost led to disaster. After the incident with the soldier, I went to a place where people went to socialize. I met a man and we started speaking in German. It was very powerful and that surprised me. Basically, it was stupid. After we spoke for a while, I realized the danger and asked him not to speak German anymore. Again, he understood, and to my relief stopped. AMAZING! (Julius and I never spoke German together. We were very grateful, Julius and I, in particular for France and what it meant to us.)

I stayed with the Brossard family for about six months. I was then fortunate to get a job as a cook (what, me cooking again?!) for the *garderie* where my children were staying. That was even more difficult. I had to split wood with an ax. I had no experience or skill; it was lucky that I did not split my own leg. It was very cold and I then had to light a huge stove with the wood, which was wet and much too large. I certainly did not succeed as it was too cold. I slept with my coat on.

An old woman was staying there with her grandson. She was very cold and huddled next to the stove which I did not manage to light. During the night she passed away and I was guilt stricken, thinking I had caused her death. The next night she appeared in my dreams and accused me of killing her by my inefficiency. I felt really bad.

There were repeated bombing incidents, which required us going down to the shelter with the twenty-two children of the *garderie*. It was scary. One time, the bombing combined with a violent thunderstorm and created havoc. It was quite something, the bombing and the thunder. It was totally overwhelming. It seemed like the whole earth was shaking. Almost like an earthquake.

The attacks got more frequent, so I decided to get away to a more secluded place. We went to a suburb of Brive, and settled there in a school. We lived in the parish classroom and I met the priest. He was very nice to me until the day I told him I was Jewish. From that day on, he never spoke to me again. Here I thought I had found a friend . . . The ground always seemed to skip under my feet.

I had left all my belongings in Brive-la-Gaillarde, in a very large trunk. I realized that this being a time of war, it would probably be pilfered and I would lose everything. So I determinedly set out, all alone, to try and retrieve it. As I walked through the woods on this long trek, I was surrounded by flying bullets. It was a miracle I did not get hit. It took me three to four hours to get there. Fortunately, my belongings were still safe, so I left them for future retrieval. At this point I do not specifically remember how I got back but I tend to believe that I did not walk back. I do not recall some of the subsequent events.

I first became a cook. As we know by now, that was not my strong suit, so I was quickly reassigned to help with the children.

Mademoiselle Monteil's mother always wanted to play tricks on us, just for fun. I was already in constant fear and did not need anyone to play BOO tricks on me at this time in my life!

By then, Richard was two and Robert four. Everyone was jammed in close quarters and a child once got head lice; it spread like wildfire among all the population. Getting rid of them was another story . . . Even I was affected. To get rid of them I had to pour gasoline over my hair as well as the children's. We all had to get our hair cut very short to stop the rapid spread. Combs made of bone with very close teeth were used to comb our hair out and remove the lice and the eggs.

A Mother's Anxiety

What do my sons remember of this time? I never wanted them to remember too much. My general outlook is that I always pushed all unpleasant and disagreeable things to the back of my mind. My approach has always been positive—make the best of all situations. I believe that otherwise, psychologically, I would not have survived. The stress was so extreme.

Robert got along better with people because he knew it was good for all of us. Richard had more of a mind of his own, and sometimes suffered the consequences. Now things are very different! Quite the opposite!

I think that Robert never wanted to remember anything, while Richard, being younger, may remember a little of that time. Robert especially has taken on this trait. He wants to pretend that we have been here in the United States forever. He does not seem to have confronted his past. Why should he when he feels comfortable? Richard, on the other hand, always likes to know things.

Hard to believe, but during our ordeal, although they were both very young, they were both very calm and quiet. Obviously, they were taking their cue from me. They never gave away our cover. I feel that this was remarkable considering their age.

> More than once, Cecile credited her children with her survival: pregnancy saved her from the Paris Velodrome round-up, and the impending birth of her first son motivated her to flee Paris during the bombing raids. Her love for them fueled her will to endure so much and to persevere. Still, she regretted their experience of so much peril when they were very young, and she hoped they did not much remember it.
>
> She described the children's strength and her daring with the following anecdote.
>
> While trudging through forested Correze, she needed to obtain food. She hoped to emerge from the woods briefly to approach a farm, but

believed that having young ones in tow would slow her and risk discovery. With few options before her, and hungry mouths to feed, she made a desperate choice: she secured one child to a tree and implored him to stay quiet in the shadows of the forest until her return. Then, stealthily, anxious as much for his well-being as for her own all the while, she crept to the farm to find sustenance.

Each step was burdened by unimaginable stress, but the goal of survival propelled her forward. "It was the safest thing to do. I hope he does not remember that." Retelling this story, she was matter of fact, as always, but not without emotion: the relief she felt when she returned and found the boy unharmed was as profound as the worry she carried in her heart during their ordeal.

Refugees in Postwar France

Things were very difficult after the war, with the unconditional surrender of the Nazis in May 1945: housing (because of the bombings), food, and other resources were scarce. There were ration tickets for basic food items for several years after the war. On the other hand, it was never that hard to find wine . . .

The end of the war did not mean that troubles were over. Prejudices were not ended by the Allies' victory. All of Europe was in an economic recession due to having to cope with the aftermath of the war. French citizens were trying to rebuild their lives and some expressed rage toward the Germans. The social fabric of the whole continent was disrupted. Refugees from many countries had to find their way back home and pick up the pieces of their lives or what was left of them. It was difficult for the Jewish survivors looking for family members, especially for those returning home after the concentration camps were liberated. At this point, many refugees and survivors did not know the fates of their relatives. Some experienced the sweetness of reunions, but for others it was a time of searching and grief. I had lost my mother, my aunt, and, of course, my Julius. People had to navigate in a whole new environment consisting of economic struggles for everyone and social conflict about who was a winner or a loser in the war.

At some point, when the German presence started to fade away, I decided to go back to the house I had been renting in Epinay-sur-Seine.

In Eyrein, I dug up my (official) *livret de famille*, which I still have, and took back my identity. Once again, I had to teach my children that their real name was Wasserman and not Lugaud. I left the children behind in Eyrein with the

Lacroix family and went to look over the situation. It was a very long and ardu-
ous trip. I had to change trains in Tulle.

I knew there was somebody living at 11 Ave Questroy, in the house where
all my furniture and belongings were. Of course, rent had not been paid by me
or the current tenants during the war, but that was OK.

Once I arrived, I found Mr. and Mme Lugaud, whose name I had used during the war, living with their child in the house. They were from the north of
France. I tried to reclaim the house where I had lived, but they would not move
out. Initially, Mme Lugaud was very friendly and tried to accommodate me;
but she refused to budge. I actually moved in and stayed in one of the smaller
bedrooms.

Mme Lugaud's parents were friends of neighbors across the street, the
Berthiaux family; it was they who had allowed the Lugauds to move in during
the war. The Lugauds stayed there rent free, and when it came time to ask them
to move out the true character of Mme Lugaud was revealed. She took me into
her confidence and told me how she constantly met all kinds of men in different places and how they were crazy about her. I knew this was not the case as
she was not a very beautiful woman. Then she went to the mayor of Epinay and
told her that I was a refugee without rights, and that she had a right to stay in the
house because she was French and I was German. She was taking advantage of
my status. I was called in to see the mayor, who asked me about the situation. I
told the mayor the facts and that was the end of that.

Then Mme Lugaud launched rumors about me in Epinay, concerning the
fact that I was a German with no rights. Mme Berthiaux, my neighbor, personally went to each house, knocked on all the doors, and flatly told people they
had to stop the rumors about me. When Mme Berthiaux came to my rescue
and took action, it was effective and the tide was turned. She and her husband
were my complete support throughout my two stays there. Having them there
was like a safe port. I could always depend on them regardless of what I needed.
Sometimes, she and I would go to Paris for dinner or just coffee. She was truly
like a mother to me.

Still, for a while I lived with the Lugaud family and I was determined to get
them out. It was most unpleasant and there was always COLD leftover food for
me. Eventually they moved up north and I got my house back.

(This reminds me that there was a young German Jewish woman living in
Epinay before the war. Once the rumors started flying about Germans and their
being spies, she committed suicide as she could not deal with it all.)

Now I need to speak about the Berthiaux family. They had befriended
Julius and me years earlier when we lived in Epinay. I was like a daughter to

them as they had lost their daughter from meningitis. At some point they lent us ten thousand francs. Once I was back and got a job, I repaid them within a few months. They always told me they had confidence in me and could trust me.

Many times, during my peregrinations, I was given a job as a cook, something I did not enjoy and was not good at doing. Nevertheless, it helped me and my children survive. At some point, certain neighbors even came over and wanted to teach me French stenography so I could get a good job.

Once I settled into the house, I had to find a way to be employed so I could support my children and myself. At first, a Jewish organization helped me with financial support. Realizing that I had marketable skills, as I was fluent in English, French, and German, I applied for a job with the American forces. I was immediately rejected because I was German-born and there were no exceptions to this rule.

Again, my friend Mme Duchenes, who had been part of the Maquis, with contacts in many places, came to my rescue. When I approached her with my plight, she spoke to an American colonel, who happened to be Jewish. Somehow, between the two of them, I was hired. What a relief! The pay was good. I worked in a nice office on Ave Kleber, off the Champs-Élysées in Paris. I had a very long commute. I took the train, the bus, and then the Métro. But it was all worthwhile as I loved my job. I also got a wonderful lunch for the princely sum of ten francs, a big bonus in those days of food rationing. On the market, a lunch would cost about two hundred francs.

Cecile, after WWII

I was hired as a secretary. From being a secretary speaking English, French, and German, I soon became much more than that. I was clever in many ways and came to use my inside knowledge of the organization and the people involved. My job was to "do whatever was necessary." I was mostly a translator, but my duties spilled over into helping people in many different ways. I creatively adapted letters in my files to a particular situation and it all worked very well. By the time I had been there for a while I had become the institutional memory. I had a wonderful relationship with everyone in the office, despite the constant rotation.

They were so lovely to me. Every morning there was candy for my children on my desk, and there were many different kind gestures. They could not believe my story. They were so wonderful, although they were all about ten years younger than me. Once, I brought Richard there and he sang for them. He had a nice voice and sang French songs. It was a lovely time for us all.

I particularly remember Lieutenant Hadley, my supervisor. She was a charming woman and for some reason she was there for a long time. We became friends; she took me out to lunch at the PX (post exchange) and for rides in her jeep. How exhilarating! I stayed on the job for two years and really liked it. (When I received my immigration papers for America, I resigned. I must say they were sorry to see me go. I remained friends with Lieutenant Hadley, and we corresponded for about two years after I left.)

While at work for the American forces, I kept getting anonymous phone calls from a man who wanted to meet me; he claimed he needed to speak with me on official business and that he was a government employee. This was very ominous. I knew deep in my heart that he was harassing me and that it was not official business. I sensed that he was against foreigners.

I even wondered if he had been put up to it by Mme Lugaud. I kept putting him off until two days before my departure for the United States. When he showed up at my house, this man was very nasty and I had a terrible argument with him. He was definitely not there on official business! I was lucky that Mr. Berthiaux was there to protect me.

Because I had to work, during the week my sons stayed with a neighbor. They were with me on the weekends. It turned out that only Robert got along with her. Richard?—no! One day, she hit Richard and he arrived home with a swollen cheek. I was shocked and I took them away immediately; it was the end of that situation.

Christine, the wife of my cousin Raymond Wasserman, knew somebody with whom the boys could stay. The only problem was that it was in the country and too far for me to see them every week. So, I would go every two weeks. I soon realized that Richard was very unhappy, so I looked around for an alternative. I brought them back with me and for a while they were across the street at Le Paradou des Enfants, a day care. They did not like that either. Nothing like being with your parents!

I was very resourceful, but it took me only so far. My relatives wanted us to come to the United States so they could help us.

I salute Mr. Blum, the prime minister of France at the time. He was Jewish. He promulgated a law creating a special passport for German refugees who at this point were stateless. I got one of those documents: it acted like a passport in most ways, and visas could be officially obtained with it. The children got a French passport because they were both born in France. Once I had secured three sponsors, all relatives, I was able to start the first important steps to apply for immigration to the United States. Uncle Fritz, my father's brother who lived in New York, and his wife Selma sponsored me; then Aunt Paula (my mother's sister) and her husband Uncle Ludwig.

It took a long time for me to obtain a visa. When that happened, I sold everything and said my goodbyes to all the wonderful people who had helped me along the way. I asked the Americans I worked with whether we should go by airplane or boat. They recommended the boat because at that time it was the safest.

First, we got train tickets from Paris to Le Havre, and then boat tickets from Le Havre to New York. My aunts paid for the tickets, which allowed us to reach the US and my supportive family. Mme Berthiaux came with us to Le Havre. I am eternally grateful to her for having done that. It was a difficult time for us. Having a friend there was such a comfort. I also met my cousin Walter in Le Havre, and that was also helpful as he was a familiar face. Although we never cried, we were touched by the moment.

Mr. and Mme Berthiaux, my neighbors and best friends who were like parents for me, were sad to see us leave. We were sad, too. Separation from good friends and family was not easy.

My children and I embarked on our new adventure and new life. That was 1947.

Shortly after I left, I heard that burglars came into the Berthiaux house and beat them up. I am sad to say that Mr. Berthiaux was blinded during that incident.

6

New Realities / Diane

My brother Alain was nine years old when we boarded the ship bound for Italy. He always had an excellent memory and still does. In a recent conversation with my sister-in-law Zippy, he shared his memories of the voyage from Egypt across the Mediterranean Sea: we passed Stromboli Volcano. We went through the Strait of Messina between Sicily and Calabria. We anchored in Naples at night. Everyone was asleep, but he was awake and looking through the porthole. He saw a huge American aircraft carrier anchored there, illuminated, with many airplanes on the deck, probably the Sixth Fleet. We disembarked in Genoa, where our father greeted us. He had been away for three months, looking for a way to settle us somewhere safe and welcoming.

Although it was not Pessah (Passover), we were out of Egypt! It was 1948.

It was very cold, and the first time we saw SNOW! I remember that my younger brother Danny and I were wearing blue coats with pockets at the breast level and there were four buttons in the front of the coats.

We went briefly to Milan, where my father had business and family connections. Crossing the Mediterranean in October, in winter clothes that we were wearing for the first time in our lives, was quite an adventure. We were shocked by the cold and the worst fog the local people had seen in many years. We now know it as smog!

None of the five children spoke Italian, so it was very difficult to adapt quickly. My sister and I would walk around, holding hands, so we would not get lost in the city.

Our father decided that we needed a break, so he took us to an expensive resort on Lake Cuomo. I remember the obsequious waiters. We then went back to Milan and visited a few historic sites. We were very impressed by a place called the Duomo. It is a large glass-enclosed building with galleries and beautiful upscale shops lining both sides. And, as a bonus, we were out of the cold . . .

We spent a couple of weeks in Italy. My parents made the decision to move on to France, as French was our native language, and hopefully my father could find work. Family helped us again: my Tante Renee, Uncle Maurice, and cousin Adam had already migrated to Paris, as well as some distant relatives and friends.

When we first arrived in Paris, we stayed at a small hotel in Saint-Mandé, in two cramped rooms, for a couple of months. We did not have a kitchen, so my mother would prepare the food on a table, and then we would take it to the bakery down the street and cook it there.

Through the grapevine, my parents heard of another old hotel at the Porte des Lillas station, which is the end of that line on the Paris Métro. Some friends and relatives from Egypt already lived there. We eventually moved to the hotel Wilson on Avenue Jean Jaures because the rooms were slightly larger. These hotels were considered "immigrant hotels."

We moved into two rooms on the eighth floor. Gisele, Joyce, and I slept in one room. My parents and my two brothers shared the room next door. They had a Murphy bed, which they opened and closed every day.

These side-by-side quarters did not connect: we entered the public hallway and knocked on the other door to be with the rest of our family. All of the tenants with rooms on that floor shared a common toilet a few doors away from ours. Quite a comedown from the lodgings we'd had back in Egypt.

Life as an Immigrant

Mornings were hectic. The worst part was bathing. We were used to bathing every day, which now became quite a challenge. Each of the rooms had a kitchenette with a stove and a sink. The girls' room was used for cooking and the other for washing up: in my parents' kitchenette, we heated water on the stove. Then we stood in a metal tub while we scrubbed and rinsed ourselves. Remember, there were five children! On the weekend, we went to the public baths. There, for a small fee, a person could have a hot shower in a private room.

In Paris, the Hotel Wilson, where Diane's family lived in two rooms.

We never wanted to leave! I remember the attendants always had a hard time getting us out of the baths. Also, there was an Olympic-size swimming pool, Piscine des Tourelles, near the Métro station not too far from our hotel. As we had been swimmers at the Sporting Club back home, we quickly gravitated to the competitive programs there. It became part of the bathing solution during the week.

Every morning, in the girls' room, we lifted our mattresses and their light-weight bed frames from the floor and propped them against a wall. Then we pulled our table and chairs to the center of the room, so we could enjoy our breakfast together before heading off to school or work.

My mother adapted to cooking for her large family in these very tight quarters, at the stove in the girls' room. She became creative and ran her kitchen on a shoestring budget.

Sometimes, she prepared a treat of homemade yogurt, which would taste better than store bought. She placed the starter in small custard cups, and filled them with warm milk. Then she arranged the cups on a metal tray. She set the tray atop the radiator for several hours or overnight until the yogurt was ready to serve.

There was no refrigeration. In Egypt, we had an ice box and regular ice delivery. Our Paris kitchenette had a small window where my mother installed a shelf. In the winter, when the weather was cold enough, she stored food in the window; everyone did. In the main room, meanwhile, there was a floor-to-ceiling window that opened onto a small railing, not quite large enough to be considered a balcony. My mother hung her plants there, and also placed a collapsible rack in the window for drying the wash. Sometimes the laundry froze or became rain-soaked: we had to bring the clothes in and hang them over the door frame.

We had very little storage space and no pantry. The children pitched in by running errands. To fetch the groceries, we trudged down and up the eight flights of steps (the hotel elevator often did not work). I remember walking to the center of the little town to fill the milk pail and the wine bottles in the stores. You would give the bottles to the wine seller, and he would fill them from the tap on a cask. The best part of these outings: the bakery was a half-block away, with bread fresh from the oven three times a day!

Despite all the handicaps in the kitchen, my mother would never let a Jewish holiday go by without inviting anyone who had no place to go. With the mattresses against the walls and three borrowed tables shoved together in the center of the room, we sat shoulder to shoulder with family and guests, eating her wonderful food and having terrific discussions. Sometimes there were twenty people in our little room during the holidays.

One holiday occasion that we remember fondly involved the dishes. We all had chores and we particularly hated washing dishes. So, a schedule was devised: the siblings took turns, with each assigned a day. One holiday, it was my turn and the dishes were piled high. I was very upset. So, I washed a few and hid the others here and there under the counters, which had curtains in front. I hung around in the kitchen and let the water run. After a decent interval, I returned to the dinner party. The next morning, my mother searched for the missing dishes and found them. I was roundly scolded. However, it was no longer my day to wash dishes, so the next person had to do them! This became a joke shared by family and guests.

We relished these special occasions, and not just for the obvious reasons and spiritual importance. The camaraderie and laughter, if just for one night, helped quench our thirst for social connection and a sense of belonging. In France, guests never showed up at your door uninvited, as they did in Egypt. It was difficult to make friends, and acquaintances never invited you to their homes: in those times of rationing, entertaining was not a top priority. Our living circumstances, seven of us in two rooms, discouraged us from inviting friends over.

Our new life was challenging. We found ourselves immersed in a totally different culture, but we were very fortunate that French was our native language. Socially, our few friendships were mostly with other immigrants from Egypt (who also spoke French). We were delighted when family friends Fortunee and Jacques Schettewi (who worked for the UN) came to Paris, as it was a treat to visit with people we knew and loved. They had a decent apartment, so we were invited for coffee and visits. Gisele and I babysat for their daughters. We stayed friends with Fortunee and her family for many years. (Fortunee passed away in 2018.)

One incident which sticks out in my mind took place every year on the first of May. On that day, many people got on their bikes and rode to the countryside. They came back with bouquets of heavily scented lilies of the valley and rang their bicycle bells. All new to me and the flowers were quite exotic. That was 1949.

Another treat that I remember. On the way home from school, a stop at the bakery for a pain au chocolat was de rigueur. We had to make a mad dash to be there early before they ran out. Always made fresh every day, it is a sophisticated, delicious French puff pastry with a stick of chocolate on one side within.

Seeking Refuge in Education

In time, we settled into the rhythm of school and work in Paris.

My father tried to reestablish his import-export business, even though he lacked a warehouse and local contacts. He had maintained contacts with suppliers in Scotland and England with whom he'd previously worked. He continued traveling on business, looking for customers who might order imported fabrics through him. By working for himself, he avoided for a while the exploitation that many other immigrants reported. Aware that an immigrant needed a job to acquire residency papers, and that residency papers were often needed to get a job, some employers took advantage. Some offered pitiful wages, well below a level commensurate with a worker's experience and knowledge. Desperate, many immigrants took those jobs.

We saw his struggles up close. Through the hardest of times, he taught us to hold our heads up high. As I grew to understand the vulnerability of life as an immigrant, I also steeled my resolve to succeed. I always say I was never a teenager: I was fourteen when we arrived in Paris, but my anxieties did not mirror those we might associate today with preening or grouchy teenagers. How could I be concerned about my hair, or a private room, when our very existence was at stake? In our cramped quarters, my sisters and I quarreled over our few possessions and lack of personal space. Recalling a childhood in which household help was taken for granted, we joked sometimes about finding rich husbands to whisk us away to lives of luxury.

Our parents insisted that we accept our new reality and acquire skills so that we could take care of ourselves. School provided an outlet for the energy, creativity, and tensions overflowing our two rooms. My parents instilled in us their belief that the girls as well as the boys must be educated to get ahead, whatever the future might bring.

At first, they enrolled us in a small school near the hotel. I remember that the classroom had a potbellied stove, which we students had to stoke. My older sister shares this memory: When it was announced at the school that new students from Egypt would be arriving the next day, a teacher told the children that we would be wearing *gallabeyas*, the traditional, free-flowing long robes worn by poor farmers. We would be barefoot, they were told. Imagine their surprise when we showed up looking just like them—in Western garb and wearing shoes!

At school, I quickly discovered I was way behind in French language and literature. One of the teachers called my mother in and told her I could take lessons after school for a fee, as she tutored children. Of course, it was out of the question; we could not afford it. The following week, the teacher invited me to come to her apartment to take the class at no cost. She saw that I was working very hard, not like her other private students, and she felt I could benefit. For her, I would be just an extra student, not a burden. She told my mother that I could motivate the lazy ones. As a teenager, I felt so good about that.

My teacher's apartment fascinated me: I had not been inside a French home, and did not know what to expect. I remember she took pride in her wooden floors, polished to a brilliant shine and buffed constantly by family and visitors, who were expected upon entering to remove their shoes and slip on a style of sandal or scuff that we called *patins*, which is "skates" in French.

Gisele recalls another teacher, one who was unsatisfied with the ramrod straight penmanship we had learned in the British-style schools in Cairo. French schoolchildren practiced a slanted handwriting style. That teacher set out to reform us. I know my handwriting never recovered!

In Paris during those years, we belonged to a scouting organization, Maccabee, just as we had back in Egypt. I was one of the senior leaders. On weekends, we ventured out together to play sports or explore the city and its surroundings. French scouts are given a special name. Mine was Myrtle or Myrtye in French.

One fateful day, our scout group met in the school yard at the lycée (high school). When we arrived, we noticed a construction project near the center of the yard, taped off to indicate danger. Logs and large concrete blocks lay haphazardly in the construction zone. The leaders warned the younger scouts to stay away. Naturally, while the leaders were busy somewhere nearby, the smaller children found the forbidden site irresistible.

My youngest brother, Danny, who was ten and ever curious, was among them. He was known in our family as the one who would wander: on the beach in Alexandria during the summer, we formed search parties and other sunbathers joined us in shouting his name, looking for the little naked boy (he loved to remove his bathing suit) up and down the length of the shore.

As the children explored the construction area, a concrete boulder came loose from its wooden supports. When it fell, it crushed one of Danny's legs. What a scene of mayhem! The school was closed, so the children and leaders sought help in the neighborhood around the school and tried to rescue him themselves!

Needless to say, I felt responsible, as I was one of the leaders. The adults repeatedly told me that I'd had nothing to do with the accident, but Danny's tragedy caused me many sleepless nights. How could we fathom what he was going through?

My brother stayed in the hospital in Paris at first. Later, he was sent to a sanatorium in Berck for rehabilitation. Berck is on the Normandy coastline north of Paris, facing the English Channel. Since the late 1800s, there have been health communes and medical centers in Berck. Good fresh air and excellent care helped restore Danny. Once, our friends Fortunee and Jacques drove us to Berck to see him. There were about fifty children in his unit, but being a loner, he did not make friends. He somehow managed to get along, and seemed always to be in good spirits when family members visited. We saw his stoicism and fortitude.

Our poverty compounded the already agonizing situation: lacking transportation, it was almost impossible to visit him in Berck. Yet we did not want him to feel abandoned.

Over time, he endured at least ten operations, with bone and skin grafts as well as metal pins, to stabilize and rebuild his leg. He would not come home for four years.

While Danny convalesced, we soldiered on. The younger children continued their studies at the suburban school. I traveled by subway to attend the Lycée Voltaire. There, I took secretarial courses such as shorthand (in French), typing, and bookkeeping, as well as the academic subjects. Because I was bilingual, I was frequently invited to visit the English class to work with the teachers and to speak with the students. That was really fun. On Thursdays, when school was half day, we could come in during the afternoon and do chemistry experiments. I loved that and wanted to be a chemist. It was not meant to be. Like my older sister before me, I put my dreams aside and went to work to help with my family's finances.

This did not end my education, however. "You never stop learning," my parents said. Somewhere along the way, my mother announced that all the girls had to enroll in continuing education classes after work or school. Even when we were tired, we went, because she joined us. We rode the subway all the way across the city to a trade program near the Champs-Élysées for classes in advanced sewing and tailoring, cooking, and embroidery. I personally liked the cooking classes.

Exhausted at the end of the evening, we would drag ourselves back to Avenue Jean Jaures, to our hotel-home. Getting up early the next morning was very difficult.

My sewing skills came in handy. My first job in Paris was in a sweatshop. I was sixteen years old and still attending the lycée. I worked in a room by myself, in somebody's apartment, sewing sleeves into the armholes of coats and jackets. I was paid by the piece, which motivated me to become very fast. It was boring, and I hated it, but it helped with the family expenses.

Languages Open Doors

Later I got a job with the NATO forces who had commandeered various estates at the end of the war and used them for office space. The office was in a mansion on the Rue de la Faisanderie, a very posh street right off the Champs-Élysées, three doors down from the home of the Duke and Duchess of Windsor. There was plenty of gold leaf, fancy wallpaper, very high ceilings, and marble. Tall glass doors opened onto exquisite gardens. With a room all to myself, it was like working in a palace.

As a secretary and typist, I answered the phones and typed many forms, often having to make ten copies of each. Believe me, I quickly became an expert and fast typist. Who wanted to place small sheets of paper under the carbons, erase the mistakes and pray the overtyping would work? I became so fast that I beat every other secretary working there, even the old-timers.

While working at this job, I lost my British accent—deliberately. All the GIs made such fun of the way I talked. To avoid the teasing, I made the effort to speak American English. I wish now that I had that British accent back. It sounds so sophisticated!

My boss, Mr. Handy, an American civilian working for NATO, introduced me to many American traditions, including jazz music. He was African American, and he knew many of the artists and musicians who lived in Paris at that time. Once, he took me along to have dinner at the home of his friend Lionel Hampton, the famous vibraphonist. Our hosts were very gracious; and after serving a wonderful meal, Mr. Hampton played for us.

At work, my output was excellent, so after a while I asked for a raise and promotion. Mr. Handy and the bosses wanted to give them to me, but they said they did not have a position open. I liked the people and the environment, but felt I deserved better. They kept putting me off, asking me to wait for a position to open up.

After a few months, I gave up on getting a promotion and searched for another job through the personnel office. Mr. Handy actually helped me find a position as a secretary and translator for the French military police and NATO. My new job was at Blériot, an historic French airplane factory located outside of Paris next to a military installation called Camp des Loges. The facility was used at that time by the American forces. The commute was longer, but I received a pay raise. Later, I learned that my former coworkers could not keep up with the work at my old job, and that I had been replaced by two people full-time and one part-time. So much for waiting for a position to open!

At Blériot, instead of working in a posh office by myself, I had a desk in a large room where there were many desks crammed together. Mme Lucienne was the office manager. She gave me a typewriter and documents to type. When she learned I was totally bilingual, she gave me assignments to translate documents from French to English, and English to French.

Mme Lucienne appeared to be low-key, but she operated with a smile and an iron fist. Nobody crossed her, not even the commanding officer. She was unusual, almost mysterious: she had wispy hair and piercing dark eyes you could not and should not avoid. At that time, she referred to herself as a mulatto, a person of mixed heritage, although the specifics of her ancestry were not discussed. With a slender build, she gracefully swung her frame on the very high heels she always wore—I always wondered how she did that.

She was a very smart and knowledgeable lady, and I soon learned that she looked out for me. She liked my work and we got along very well. I had great respect for her. She rescued me from an embarrassment of my own making: when I filled out my application for the job, I indicated that I could take stenography dictation. I failed to mention, however, that I could take dictation in French only! My first assignment in English was, mercifully, a short letter. Mme Lucienne quickly assessed the situation, and stepped in.

Coming of Age in Paris

Although the officer wanted the new young secretary with the gorgeous legs to take dictation, Mme Lucienne would announce that she had a different job for me to do. Then she took the dictation. Believe me, she was a whiz at it! Eventually, my skills improved. On many occasions, I translated documents for two French detectives assigned to the military police (MP) office. Mr. Merceron and Mr. Mercier were liaison officers between the MPs and the French police. They investigated alleged crimes involving American servicemen in France, and basically greased the wheels as cases moved between French and American law enforcement agencies.

Frequently, they came back from investigations and regaled us with stories about arresting GIs who had destroyed a bar in a drunken rage, or committed other, more violent, offenses, such as shootings. They were two tough cops! They often worked late into the night and they expected me to stay to answer the telephone, translate documents, and type reports.

One day, Mme Lucienne announced that I was being reassigned with a promotion: I'd be accompanying the two French police officers, who were being transferred. Most of the incidents they investigated took place in Paris; it had been decided that traveling daily to Blériot was not necessary. A liaison office would be established in Paris under the auspices of the CIA in the NATO office. I would become the office manager and translator: this meant that I would help the officers interrogate suspects! I also became friends with the CIA guys next door who took advantage of my skills. Now I could say: "I am working for the CIA!" Again, Mme Lucienne had been gracious to me. I had worked there from 1955 to 1957, and I was sorry to leave.

The new office was located on Rue Marbeuf, just off the Champs-Élysées, halfway down between l'Etoile and La Place de la Concorde. Talk about a fancy neighborhood; this was two streets away from the major couture houses. Catching a whiff of high society, I took walks at lunchtime down the Champs-Élysées or went window-shopping along the small, elegant side streets. I particularly enjoyed the Dior windows. At the house of Worth, all I could see was the polished brass plate next to the huge doors—no windows! Nevertheless, I was a great fan and still wear their perfume, Je Reviens.

In these Paris streets, people from all walks of life dressed very well and creatively. Compared to the casual and often all-black, safe fashions seen today, the apparel at that time was colorful and exciting. My sisters and I took note of the styles, as did most working girls, though we usually made our own skirts and dresses. We shopped for fabric and notions at Marche St. Pierre at the foot of Montmartre and Bouchara, close to the Galleries Lafayette department store: they specialized in remnants from the couture houses. We tailored our patterns to replicate some of the looks inspired by the great designers. Rue Marbeuf was closer to home than Blériot, but still a world away from my life in two rooms of the hotel.

Getting to work was never easy. I stayed up late reading (under the covers), so I was a sleepyhead in the morning. I was frequently late and was once threatened with being fired if I did not start coming in on time. We had no car, so I had to walk several blocks from our hotel to the Métro, which was very crowded at rush hour. People pushed and shoved to get in, and you had to keep your wits about you because you could be pick-pocketed or goosed. Subway delays sent me into a tailspin, because my job was at stake. And I still had another few blocks to walk when the train pulled into the station nearest the office. It took effort on my part to become more reliable.

The office on Rue Marbeuf bustled with activity: a variety of American and NATO military offices shared the building. I quickly made friends. Some of the soldiers would take me to lunch at the cafeteria, which was for US personnel only. There, I indulged in grilled cheese sandwiches made with white bread—one of the many American treats introduced to me while I worked for the armed forces. Imagine: craving white sandwich bread in the middle of Paris, with bakeries producing great breads all around! Today, I wouldn't touch white bread with a ten-foot pole!

Other innovations from the States delivered to Parisians, with the help of the servicemen:

- Poodle skirts. These wide circle skirts made of felt were all the rage. We sewed the skirts, but you needed a friend with access to the Post Exchange who was willing to buy the crinoline that made the skirt stand out. The image of a soldier buying one of these big poufy things, and carrying it around, made me laugh. Needless to say, I was thrilled to get a couple for my sisters and myself.
- Bingo, a game which I had the opportunity to play at social functions.
- The Harlem Globetrotters—so tall and funny!
- Jitterbug and jazz bands.
- Hot dogs, American-style, with relish, mustard, and catsup (which the French used to denigrate as a sauce Americans used to mask bad cooking).
- The wry humor of Art Buchwald, whose columns in the *International Herald Tribune* entertained the homesick GIs and gave me priceless insights into American culture. I continued to read his columns for years in Paris and later in America.

Working in a military office meant I was constantly surrounded by men, an experience that was new for me. I dated some of the servicemen. Dating! That was a joke at the time. I only had a couple of dates with a guy I did not like.

Unfortunately, some of the GIs had heard that all the French girls were "loose" and assumed that the rumors had merit. They continuously propositioned me. I was flabbergasted. They would ask me to move in with them. Life would be great, they would say; I would not have to worry about rationing and they could provide for my family. What gall!

About this time, Gisele worked for a man named Rudy, the owner of a small company that sold plastic tablecloth in the Jewish quarter of Paris. She was the bookkeeper and clerical helper, and she pitched in to cut fabric and do other tasks as needed. She was poorly paid.

I encouraged her to apply at the armed forces personnel office, and the finance office hired her. We worked in the same building, though in different departments and on different floors. Gisele met her future husband there, Sheldon Prushan, a draftee from Philadelphia who also worked in the finance office.

One day, Sheldon was on the elevator when a fellow got on.

"What are you doing here?" they both blurted out.

That other man was Morton Tuckman, a childhood friend from Philadelphia, at that time a serviceman stationed at a base in the Bordeaux region, south of Paris. They had spent many summers together, as their families had vacationed at the same place in New Jersey. A decade had passed since they'd seen one another, and their chance reunion in that elevator became a fateful intersection in all of our lives.

Morton, a recent graduate of the Wharton School, was an accountant assigned to keep inventory—he always joked that it was his job to count the tanks. He frequently visited Paris, often on the weekends for entertainment and to change his money (one could get a better exchange rate for dollars on the black market in Paris than out in the countryside). Sheldon and a friend, Bob Weiss, shared an apartment and were eager to add a third person, especially one who came around only on the weekends but still paid his share.

As I mentioned earlier, my mother had to invite the whole world for the Jewish holidays. Sheldon, by then, was a regular visitor to our "home." He introduced Morton to us as his new roommate and old pal from the States. That is how I met my future husband.

In time, we began dating. Sometimes, we would go out to hear music or see a show. Sometimes, we double-dated with Gisele and Sheldon. We would sometimes go out for an interesting evening, frequently with other buddies tagging along.

One evening we went to a restaurant called La Rotisserie de la Reine Pedauque. It was a very upscale place with an excellent reputation. (It is no

longer in business.) As one course followed another, we were served a different wine to complement the particular
dish. They considered us to be a large
group so a large bottle appeared each
time and we were encouraged to drink;
they said we were eating so we would
not get drunk, so why let it go to waste?
We had imbibed quite a large quantity
by the end of the meal and I was quite
lightheaded.

Diane's engagement portrait

With the dessert they offered coffee. I have had a longtime aversion to
coffee so I became a little silly. By the
time we left I was, shall we say, drunk.
The guys took us home and of course the elevator was not working. They recall
how they pushed me and shoved me up the eight flights of stairs while I kept
yelling about not wanting any coffee. The last part is hearsay as I do not remember much past leaving the restaurant. When I described my adventure to my
work colleagues on the following Monday, they roared with laughter. I still do
not drink coffee!

Morton and I took long walks and held hands. In the front of Notre Dame
sits a bench where Morton and I would kiss and hug. To my surprise, that land-
mark bench was still there, in that spot, many years later; seeing it sparked memories of our long-ago courtship, which was slow, as he lived in the Bordeaux
region and came just for the weekend.

I remember one day we were sitting on that bench smooching when he
proposed. He did not give me a ring . . .

Seeking Opportunity

After nine years in Paris, my family saw there was no way we could improve
our circumstances. My father could not advance and lacked the resources to
build his import business into a success. The papers required for residency and
work permits remained elusive. Had he obtained them, finding any housing
would have been difficult: in postwar Paris, the population exploded and
housing remained scarce and expensive. We had no family connections. We

felt futureless, so to speak. Through friends, we heard that Canada was open to immigrants, so we applied to emigrate as a family.

Giselle decided to stay in France to be with Sheldon. That year, they married in a civil service at Paris city hall, as they had the time to do the paperwork for her to go to America. The following year, when they moved to the United States, they repeated their vows in a Jewish wedding ceremony, this time for real. What I am trying to say is that in their eyes they were not really married, only as a convenience so she could move to the United States as a dependent. We attended their wedding ceremony in Philadelphia and I was a bridesmaid.

It was 1958. Morton's tour of duty in France was coming to an end while my family was waiting for immigration papers to move to Canada. He managed to extend his enlistment for six months, so we could be together for a while longer. We were by then engaged. We began making our wedding plans, which would be complicated by international travel and immigration regulations.

Our strategy was that I would get a tourist visa to the United States and see how we would deal with the situation. We planned to stay with my in-laws for two or three weeks in Philadelphia, until Morton's employer, the Internal Revenue Service in Wilmington, Delaware, assigned him to begin a new job in Georgetown, Delaware, where we would officially put down our first roots as a married couple.

Meanwhile, preparing to leave France, I sewed my gown. The fabric was a heavy white cotton shot with silver thread. The dress was fitted at the waist and then straight down. I needed only a hat and a veil. I would also wear a double strand of pearls that my mother had given me for the occasion. Preparing to leave home for the unknown of another country, this time I packed to be a bride, not just a wayfarer in a new land.

My husband planned to arrange our wedding in Montreal to coincide with the time when I would arrive in Canada.

I was quite friendly with a lady who worked in the police liaison office in Paris. One day, she announced that she and her boyfriend were emigrating to Canada. It was a surprise to me. When she heard of our plans, she let me know that as soon as I came to Montreal, she would help Morton organize the wedding. I just could not believe such luck. A few months later, Morton contacted her from the US, and indeed she was ready to follow up on her commitment.

Our departure from France in 1959 had none of the drama of our original exit from Egypt. As a family, we boarded a steamship at Le Havre (the same port from which Cecile left France for America). Bad weather marred the voyage: I was seasick for the entire trip. It was September. The skies did not clear until we were approaching Montreal. Friends of our parents, who lived in an apartment building in Montreal, helped us find a place to stay.

A Wedding in Montreal

While I was seasick on the boat, Morton traveled to Montreal and our acquaintance helped with all the details. She also came to the wedding. I was most grateful, as we did not know the city or very many people.

After we arrived in the city, I met up with Morton and we arranged to meet with the rabbi and publish the bans, which at that time involved posting your announcement at the synagogue door to announce the wedding, in keeping with traditional French law.

I met my in-laws on the day of my wedding, September 25, 1959, one week after we docked in Montreal. My father-in-law, Herman Tuckman, was well connected in Philadelphia. He had worked for the Philadelphia Health Department and had also held a brief appointment with the Free Library. He also later served as secretary for the Civil Service Employee's Association, and worked to have white collar workers accepted into the CIO (the Congress of Industrial Organizations). He was a sweetheart. My mother-in-law was more of a problem. She had all the hang-ups of survivors of the Depression: always felt that she had the short end of the stick.

Most of the guests were family members, about twenty people all together. A few friends from Egypt who had moved to Canada before us were also there.

The simple wedding ceremony set the stage for the next adventure of our lives. We planned to set out for Morton's home in the United States the same day, immediately after the reception, in a Volkswagen Bug that Morton had shipped over from Germany.

My father-in-law would accompany us for the drive south, as we feared being stopped at the border. I had obtained only a tourist visa, so it would raise suspicions to try to enter the United States as a newlywed couple. Traveling as a threesome, however, we could say that Mr. Tuckman had invited me for a visit. We planned to cross into the United States, drop off my father-in-law at the nearest Greyhound Bus terminal, and continue south to Philadelphia.

In those heady hours just after reciting our wedding vows, we drove to the border with my bridal bouquet hidden under the seat.

At the checkpoint, I held my breath. The US Customs and Immigration agents looked us over, examined our papers, asked a few questions, and waved us through. Whew! The highlight of my wedding day was getting into America without a hassle.

And so began our honeymoon—departing Montreal and sightseeing from upper New York State down through Pennsylvania, stopping at landmarks, and enjoying the dappled fall forests, mountains, and lakes.

For our wedding, relatives did not know what presents to give us, as we had not yet established ourselves. Although we received many nice presents when we got to Philadelphia, several friends and family did not know what to give us and gave us money. We used some of it to buy a NECCHI sewing machine, one of the first machines that did embroidery designs. I still own it. In my family tradition, it helped me sew fabulous outfits (I always looked well dressed) and make curtains for the apartment. Just like my mother, I had foreseen the necessity of having a sewing machine. I had a small allowance to buy what I wanted for myself, and sewing certainly allowed me to extend the allowance.

It was a cultural shock for me when a couple of weeks after my wedding we were invited to the wedding of one of Morton's cousins. At some point, the bride took me aside and wanted to look at my ring. She was shocked that I did not have one . . . She asked me when were we leaving for our honeymoon to Florida? When I said that we'd just come back from our honeymoon traveling from Montreal to Philadelphia, she was speechless. It was as though I were not married, according to the local "traditions" in America at that time!

After our honeymoon, we discovered that I would have to go back to Canada and apply for an immigration visa. That could take several months. More twists and turns.

At that time, Herman, my father-in-law, was employed for the Philadelphia Health Department; and it is likely that through his job he worked closely with the Philadelphia mayor's office. The mayor at that time was Joseph S. Clark. He became one of Pennsylvania's senators in January of 1957, and served in this role through January of 1969. It is possible that Herman contacted Clark to assist in my case. Senator Clark was in a position to introduce a private immigration bill on my behalf, although my name wasn't mentioned in the document. It became Public Law 86-648 on July 14, 1960, and it offered authorizations for refugee resettlement in the US under certain conditions. I fell under one of the conditions and obtained US residency.

7

Coming to America / Cecile

Au Revoir, France

In February 1947, at Le Havre, my children and I boarded a converted warship, the USS Washington, for the transatlantic crossing to New York. Being an opera buff, I equated this ship with *The Flying Dutchman* by Wagner. It was not yet fully converted, so the lights were dim and it had an unusual feeling about it. We shared a cavernous cabin with about thirty women. Some of them were dressed in exotic outfits, like something out of *The Arabian Nights*. They moaned, groaned, and cried, adding an eerie feeling to the whole adventure.

Now about the weather . . . It was horrible, whipping up huge waves. Soon after departure, the sea got very bad and almost everyone was sick, including me. Early on, I met a lovely tall Swiss woman. When I got very unwell, she took over the care of the children, for which I was most grateful. At the beginning, the children ate and the Swiss lady remained healthy, until the end when everybody, including her and the staff, as well as the boys, became very seasick. As the ship rocked, everything fell off the tables and broke (including our perfume bottles). I had so looked forward to decent food during the crossing, after being deprived for so long in France. But it was not meant to be.

The children and I felt poorly until we disembarked. We were all so happy to get off that boat! Because of the weather, we arrived twenty-four hours late. My aunt and uncle who were there to greet us had waited for us all that time.

We arrived in New York on a Tuesday morning at 8:00 a.m., but we could not leave the ship until 4:00 p.m. Strict inquiries were made before anyone was allowed to disembark. It was extremely difficult for everyone. While waiting, we lined up for tea. People were so hungry that they were putting lemon, sugar, and milk in their tea, so it curdled.

We were warmly greeted by several of my relatives, including some from Julius's side of the family whom I had never met. It was very heartwarming. Once we disembarked and all the formalities were taken care of, we drove off through the heavy snow to Toms River, NJ, where Aunt Paula and Uncle Ludwig lived. It was all quite bewildering.

Three weeks later, I was introduced to Henri Spiegel. He was also from Germany. He was already a published author in Germany on the subject of small gardens. In the 1930s, the American ambassador to Germany, a graduate of Cornell, had given him a very fast visa to the United States and instructed him to go there immediately as the semester had already started. That is how he got out of Germany. By the time I met Henri, he was a professor of economics teaching at Catholic University in Washington, DC.

Henri and Cecile Spiegel, 1948

We got married and moved to the Washington area, and we temporarily left the children in Toms River with my aunt and uncle. I was separated from my children at various times. It was very hard for me and for them as well.

I only wish that Henri, my second husband, had been nicer to the children. A couple of days before we got married, he said something to the effect that he did not want the children. But there was no way my children would not be a part of my life. They were my priority. Later, he adopted them because he felt it was the right thing to do.

US Citizenship

Within my lifetime, I was born in Germany, escaped to England, got to France, and finally immigrated and settled in the United States.

I had to study American history to pass the citizenship test. I did so diligently and was ready. Indeed, I had no trouble, and on March 15, 1951, I became a US citizen. Henri and the children Richard and Robert came with me. The boys became citizens automatically on that day as well. Robert was ten years old and Richard was eight. We remember very little of this momentous event except that we were happy that the odyssey was over.

Never Forget / Cecile

I do not consider myself officially as a victim of the Holocaust because I did not experience its worst horrors first-hand, having left relatively early. But I am a victim of the fallout of the Holocaust. A way of life was lost to me when I was still quite young. My family, like many others, was beset by tragedies and much trauma.

I lost my beloved husband Julius, my mother, and her sister, my aunt Regina, in the Holocaust. (Their names are inscribed on the wall of remembrance in the Holocaust Museum in Washington, DC.)

My family also lost their properties. (My second husband, Henri, took on the responsibility of doing all the paperwork so I could receive compensation. It was a long and laborious job but he was successful and that helped me later in life.)

My uncle Bert Lehman, his wife Hilde, and their three children, my favorite cousins, immigrated to the United States well before the situation in Germany seriously deteriorated.

Of my family who had remained in Germany, only my aunt Paula and my uncle Ludwig survived—but barely. They were warned about Kristallnacht. At nightfall they got into their Mercedes and drove off to the countryside and spent the night at an inn. Quietly and surreptitiously the next day, after the men had been rounded up and it was very dark, they came back. It appears that the son of the building superintendent saw them and reported them to the Gestapo. Within the hour, they picked up my uncle. He and my aunt said they were in the process of leaving and were almost ready to go. The authorities said just let us know when you are ready to leave. Aunt Paula supervised the packing and closing of the house, as well as all the formalities concerning the tickets and papers, a monumental task for a woman alone under such circumstances. And indeed, when everything was ready, she contacted the authorities and Uncle Ludwig was delivered to the boat and they sailed off. They ended up in America.

When they were both very young, they had made a pact that when one of them died the other would follow. And, as they had promised one another, Aunt Paula died just after Uncle Ludwig. She committed suicide using the car and the garage: carbon monoxide. I was living with them in Toms River when she died. The day before, I could hear her typewriter going all day. She was typing a letter to every member of the family. I believe that she did not want to cope with being old and alone.

I am sure that in my peregrinations I was always somehow guided as to where, when, and how to go. Did I have a guardian angel watching over me? If so, I am sure it was the spirit of my mother whom I adored. I seemed to feel her presence at all times.

The Fate of Cousin Julius Wasserman

My husband's cousin, also called Julius, had a beautiful wife and two gorgeous sons. One of them, Henri, a darling young man of eighteen years old, was a sweetheart in the way he related to my small children. The other, Raymond, was an excellent swimmer. (He swam in the Seine in Paris in the dead of winter and this is how he met his wife, Christiane. They were both very *sportif*.)

When the Nazis came to Paris, Cousin Julius and his family fled to Lyon. On the way, they stopped to visit us in Eyrein in Correze. During their visit, I was touched by the fact that young Henri went to the only store in town, in Hotel Beysac, which was by the train station, and found some toys for my children. Until then, the children had had nothing to play with but my camera and pots and pans. That visit was the last time we saw Cousin Julius and his family.

In Lyon, they stayed in an apartment which belonged to a Jewish couple who'd gone into hiding. When the Nazis came to look for that other family, they scooped up cousin Julius, his wife, and Henri. Raymond was out at some sporting event and so was spared; Christiane then hid him.

Before moving to Lyon, Julius and his wife had lived in an apartment in Paris with her parents, who were both blind and in their nineties. Therefore, they were always home. After the younger Wassermans went to Lyon, the parents were caught and deported like other members of my family who became victims of the Holocaust.

9

American Odyssey / Diane and Cecile

———————

Culture Shock / Diane

When I arrived in Georgetown, Del., with Morton, it was quite a shock. I was lonely because I could not drive and did not know anyone except the next-door neighbor, her husband, and their young daughter. They were incredibly good to me. From them, I learned about American customs.

I felt totally uprooted and isolated. Georgetown had a population of only three thousand at that time, and I felt I was the oddity in town. The social structure there revolved around the town's two churches, a lifestyle which was out of the question for me. There was no synagogue to welcome me in my new community.

The second day I was there, I walked to the small local grocery store and looked to purchase fresh parsley. The store owner offered me dried parsley in the jar, and when I said no, I want fresh parsley, he asked me why. I told him that I needed it to put in my hamburger, because that is how hamburger was prepared in France. He was flabbergasted.

As I walked down the streets, I would notice the curtains being slightly drawn back as people peered out and looked at me like I was from outer space.

The supermarket was too far away to walk. Morton would drive me there. This was a totally new experience, as there had been no supermarkets in France when I lived there. There, I'd shopped daily on the street, where the stores were lined up next to each other: the meat store (including horse meat shop!), delicatessen, bakery, fresh vegetables and fruit, etc. Back in Egypt, we had shopped at the bazaar or bought groceries from strolling vendors.

Early in my marriage, it was difficult to make many cultural adjustments in my way of life. My husband was demanding. The hardest lesson I had to learn was to stand my ground. For instance, I had to ignore the suggestion from my mother-in-law to call her every day! She said that this is what everybody did in America. So, I strove very hard to maintain my independence.

My husband was on a relatively low pay scale, as he worked for the government, but he managed our financial situation very well. I received an allowance every month to use as I wished and not have to ask him for money. When I came to America, I felt I had to work, even part-time, to contribute to our meager income. This allowed us to budget for vacations. Also, it helped to counteract the loneliness and isolation.

I took a job as a saleslady in Georgetown, just as my mother had done when our family had immigrated to Canada in 1958. My mother, at the age of fifty-one, helped pay the bills. She worked in Eaton's, an upscale department store, in the handbag department. She enjoyed helping people purchase a handbag they would cherish and use for a long time. (I still own a couple of those timeless handbags.) She was my example.

There were three clothing stores in Georgetown when I moved there: a women's store, a men's shop, and a children's store, all owned by a Jewish family. They did not live in town but miles away in Salisbury, Maryland. One of Morton's friends from college also lived there, so we had the opportunity to drive all that distance to Salisbury to attend services and visit the friends.

I really loved working at the women's store, because I got to meet the people of the community, and it helped me adjust to my new surroundings. The customers gravitated to me because I was from Paris.

It was a commission job, so after a while I got very nervous because I noticed that the other salespeople were losing customers. I thanked the owners and took a position as a secretary for an attorney. After a few months, I left because my son Ian was born.

We were told to contact the mohel in the congregation in Wilmington, Delaware, to arrange for the traditional circumcision rite. We called and he set the date for the Brit Milah; and when we told him we didn't know ten Jews in Georgetown (the number of men needed for this tradition), he said, don't worry, they will be there. Sure enough, at the appointed time, several men showed up, in their boots and work clothes, carrying a bottle of wine. They told us that it was such an honor to participate in this important event. We never saw them again.

When I became a parent, I felt it was important to learn better parenting skills, because I had no family around to advise and teach me. Being an immigrant and a refugee is difficult on many different levels. Being an immigrant and a woman is even more difficult. Somehow, the support system is more fragile and frequently dispersed. We are uprooted—often knowing no one, and frequently having to deal with childbirth and family on our own without the wisdom of the patriarchs and matriarchs close by.

My mother came from Canada to help me when my son was born and stayed two weeks. For daily basic advice I relied on my next-door neighbor and her teenage daughter, who was a big help and enjoyed spending time with the baby.

Once I learned how to drive, many horizons became open to me and I took advantage of them, travelling all over the countryside. One of the pluses of being in Georgetown was that we lived twenty minutes from the beach, a place I loved from my childhood. We frequently went to the beach, and I learned about the Easter hat parade on the boardwalk, and of course participated in that.

Later, we moved to Atlantic City, New Jersey. There, I taught French in the evening to adults and became a US Census taker, which was fascinating and allowed me to feel quite integrated.

Morton was still with the Internal Revenue Service. One day, one of Morton's clients invited us to his club for a drink and a show. It turned out that the performer was Frank Sinatra! We had a front row table, and at intermission Sinatra came over and we had a nice chat. Hard to believe!

We had been there for a few months when my husband learned that they were recruiting individuals who knew the tax code to train as programmers who would place the country's tax information on computers. He had graduated from the University of Pennsylvania, where computers were developed while he was a student. He applied and was selected, and we moved to Washington, DC, in the early sixties.

We decided to live on the Maryland side of the beltway. When we were ready to buy a house, I wanted to find a Jewish community close by before we selected the house. I said, "I am tired of being a wandering Jew! Now is the time for me to set down roots and take an active part in my religious life." So we went synagogue shopping. One Saturday, we walked into the Jewish Community Center of Prince George's County, since renamed Mishkan Torah, in Greenbelt. Within ten minutes I looked at Morton, he looked at me, and the decision was made. We then found our house, which is fifteen minutes away. And it has turned out to be everything I was looking for.

This is where I lived when I heard about the Foreign Language in the Elementary School (FLES) program in Maryland. At the start of the program, French was the only language taught. This was a voluntary afterschool program sponsored by the Parent Teacher Association (PTA). The primary require-ment for the instructors was to speak French fluently with a native accent, and I certainly could do that. I also enjoyed working with children. I applied, was accepted, and started teaching in Beltsville, Maryland.

After much lobbying by the PTA, the Prince George's County Board of Education became interested in the project. They could see the value and the excellent results achieved so easily and economically. The program, then, became an official part of the curriculum.

We were not on the same pay scale as full-time teachers, and were only part-time, paid by the hour, and poorly paid. But we all loved what we were doing. Many participants taught in several schools, but I did not as by then I had young children and did not have a car. I taught only at Lamont Elementary School in Lanham, within walking distance of my house.

Later, after my daughter Valerie was born in 1963, I was able to leave her with a sitter across the street while I was teaching. My son Ian was in kindergar-ten right there where I was during the day, at Lamont Elementary School.

FLES was an innovative course structured for children in Grades four, five, and six, and involving a television program. They watched the program twice a week for twenty minutes. The French teacher then came into the classroom three times a week, with props, reinforcing the content of the previous program and continuing to build on the vocabulary taught on television. No reading or writing, just speaking. Fluency with a good accent was the goal. And it worked! This was a shoestring operation, with only one supervisor to monitor several teachers. We were required to tape a session twice a year so he could check on our effectiveness. When we listened to the tapes, it was clear how successful the whole idea was. The children mimicked us perfectly. We eventually heard from foreign language teachers in the upper grades how delighted they were with the performance of the students and how easily they progressed.

Once the program became part of the curriculum in the public schools of Prince George's County, we had to take a methodology course at the University of Maryland to qualify, as it was no longer run by the PTA. The instructor was Professor Mandes. The class was scheduled on Saturday mornings: Morton could take care of our son Ian so I was free to attend. It was a large group, with many interesting people from various countries and backgrounds. Among them were many German war brides who knew French.

This is where I met Cecile, in the spring of 1962.

I remember it was spring, because in my usual French tradition, it was time to sew up a new suit and a new light-colored spring coat. I started with the suit. I had purchased a beautiful lilac linen fabric (at the old G Street Fabrics in downtown Washington) and used an Yves Saint-Laurent designer pattern to make a lovely simple suit with interesting buttons offset to one side. I was wearing the suit and felt particularly good that day when Cecile approached me in class.

During the class, the professor had made a statement about the importance of what we were teaching: "Once you learn a language with an accent you cannot change it," he said. I immediately raised my hand. I asked him if he could tell from my accent how I had learned English. He said I had an American accent with a slight deviation. I informed him that I spoke British English in grade school but had later changed my accent in order to fit in, when the American GI's in France made fun of my accent. The class roared with laughter. The professor said, "There is always an exception to the rule, and you are it."

During that same year, I had the opportunity to take the test for American citizenship. Morton was furious that I would not study. There was no cause for worry: I passed with flying colors, mostly because I knew some obscure events in American history and, of course, by then spoke perfect English.

The morning I was to be sworn in—August 21, 1962—my husband told me that after the ceremony I could vote in the next election. I remember going to the courthouse and being sworn in as a citizen. As we were walking out of the courtroom, we were all escorted down the hall by the sheriff to a room where we were all invited to register to vote. *Immediately!* Morton and I laughed, as the official was not about to let us out before we had registered. A nice lunch followed.

My citizenship papers are ensconced in a safe location. I once had to pull them out to verify the spelling of my name as somehow it had been misspelled on my driver's license. This was the ultimate proof.

Citizenship is a prized possession at any time. After experiencing the feeling of being virtually or literally stateless for so long, at last I felt I belonged.

Still, I am reminded that at that time I was a fairly distant person. I was not quite insecure; I projected an attitude of superiority, although I did not feel superior. I was just shy and uncertain. I can certainly trace that to the fact that I was an immigrant with much to learn.

Sometimes, we are reminded in odd or funny ways how different cultures, customs, and preferences are as we cross borders and adopt local ways. Here is one example: I was delighted when, many years after I moved to America, Mr. Merceron, one of the policemen I had worked with in Paris, came to visit me with his wife. At dinner, I served broccoli to the guests. They looked at each other and nibbled at it. Eventually, they blurted out that in France broccoli was eaten by cows, not people . . .

Friendships Blossom / Cecile

By 1962, my boys had grown and left home, so I needed to do something to get over the empty-nest syndrome. Through a friend of mine, Louisa Dillard, I heard about the opportunity to teach French in elementary schools. Though I was fluent in French after living for so long in France, I was required to take a class at the University of Maryland. This was the class where Diane and I met.

I was immediately intrigued by her. She seemed to be so aloof, and yet I instinctively liked her. We didn't speak until almost the last class, but I observed her from afar. When I did finally approach her, on that lovely spring day, I discovered that she was open for conversation, and we hit it off. She told me about her family, and I told her about mine. I realized that despite differences in our backgrounds we shared many similar experiences.

When I mentioned that my husband and I had been looking for a house for two years, she invited me to lunch so I could see her new house and neighborhood in Lanham, Md. I remember the pleasant time we had. Diane is a good cook, and I enjoyed meeting her three-year-old son, Ian, with his dark velvet eyes and beautiful face. I immediately liked this neighborhood with its just-completed houses. The houses were dissimilar, with delightful well-kept yards in the front, and yards and decks in the back facing the woods of Greenbelt Park.

This was exactly what I wanted! I had found my dream neighborhood. The big question was: Would my husband like the area and find a house to his liking? I was elated that he also liked the houses. We bought one and my family often saw Diane's. I enjoyed taking her son Ian shopping with me when I ran my errands. People would ask about the little boy with the black eyes . . . but would be wondering about my blond hair and blue eyes . . . I would simply say he belongs to a friend. Of course, he returned with a small toy or trinket every time. I could not resist his requests and I enjoyed spoiling him. When Diane's daughter Valerie was born, I came to the hospital with a beautiful white dress to bring her home in. It was as though I had a close loving family around me.

That is how we became neighbors, friends, and colleagues—and we continued to teach in the FLES program for many years.

10

Reflections on Immigration

The Time of Wandering Ends / Cecile

How did I cope? With one foot in front of the other as I trudged through the French countryside, pushing my children in the pram.

I used my smarts, kept my wits about me, and remained alert. I relied on my good disposition and smiled a lot. My faith in the innate goodness of people proved to be a life saver many times over.

Diane and I are most grateful to France, which harbored us, protected us, and nurtured us, but there came a time for us to move on. We both, at different times, emigrated to America. It was not an escape, but a choice—a big difference.

As American citizens, we stop, salute the flag, and thank God we live in this amazing country. Though I lack a fine musical voice, I actually *sing* the "Star-Spangled Banner"! And, of course, this is the last stop in the immigration process for us.

We have no regrets. Any thoughts of going back? NEVER!

We constantly revisit the narrative of loss and longing—it's part of our memories. We make alibis. Consciously or subconsciously, we continuously analyze as we revisit the past with nostalgia. Storytelling helps us with the hard parts: we cheat and create a narrative which makes it interesting and exciting.

We do not actually recreate but embellish the extant conversation as we attempt to recapture the people and events. Memory does begin to flicker and fade, though the facts are the facts.

We suffered many trials and tribulations but IT WAS GOOD!

We had to find our way. With our faith intact, we braved everything that was dished out to us. We survived and we thrived. Through the immigrant experience, we came into our own, feeling valued, important, and empowered.

Go Forth! / Diane

I was a fourteen-year-old teenager when I became an immigrant for the first time. It was traumatic yet I looked forward to what I perceived to be a great adventure. I knew it would not be easy. I did not have too many dreams growing up. It was a day-to-day slog to keep my head above water, help pay the bills, have a little fun, and survive. Yet, somehow, I felt safe surrounded by my family. So, I did not look back, and in fact I must have pulled down a curtain on my previous life. I cannot remember many things about my life in Egypt. For a long time, I somehow walled myself off from the fact that we were very poor.

From a female perspective, the core of our immigration experiences have been real challenges. Despite all the traumas involved, we still consider ourselves very fortunate!

As immigrants and refugees, women frequently suffer from violence, threats, and indifference, and are tempted to abandon their moral values and lose their emotional compass. The stress of the immigration experience can lead to getting in with the wrong crowd, attempting to fit in and finding a safe haven. The promise of an easy out, comradeship, empathy, and shortcuts is quite alluring. It is hard to avoid yielding to the temptations. These can only lead to disaster and the loss of self-esteem. Cecile witnessed such situations during the war and recounted many such horror stories to me on this subject.

Also, especially in wartime, responsibility often falls to women to work long hours outside the home to help with expenses, find ways to look after the children, and keep everything in balance.

Again, our families played a leading role in keeping us right on track. No way we could embarrass or disappoint them!

During our immigration experiences, we met many people who contributed to our assimilation and whose help encouraged us to fit into a new society.

We both trusted in our ability to share our stories in a meaningful way to connect with them.

Along the way, our tried and true support systems collapsed with the changes in countries, circumstances, historical events. We persisted, and built new networks, which is one of the parallels in our life journeys.

11

Lekh-L'kha / Diane

Adonai said to Abram: "Go forth from your native land and from your father's house, to the land that I will show you. He took Sarai and they left." (Genesis 12:1).

In our case, our parents told us to "Go forth," and we went . . .

Cecile crossed borders three times. Her mother told her, "It is time for you to GO! There is nothing here for you. Your fiancé Julius, the love of your life, is already in Paris, so you need to go there." She said, "I will help you, but I am not ready to leave myself."

My family sacrificed to protect us from rising persecution, and then to find economic opportunity. We leaped not once but twice. My parents said, "It is now time to leave Egypt," and we did.

In both cases they were right.

Like Abram and Sarai, we did not know where we would go and what we would face, but we knew we needed to do this to survive physically, mentally, and spiritually. We discovered that migration is an uncontrollable force. People will find a way when they must go. And when they land, as the saying goes, they will try to bloom where they are planted.

Cecile was an adult and I was a teenager when we first left home, so we were old enough to feel that we were defined to a certain extent by our countries of origin. This is where our cultural roots are. Some of it is ingrained, while some aspects can be shed. As refugees we frequently pondered that fact.

For both of us, setting out and leaving everything behind opened new doors and worlds to us. Sometimes it felt like we were watching from the sidelines, as if our own lives were theater, with constant changes and challenges.

Survival means taking these challenges with a positive attitude and recognizing found opportunities. It also means understanding love as a source of strength. I don't really have the words to explain, but Cecile frequently touched on this, indicating that there was no wavering from this idea. She felt the power of the love and recognition heaped on her by her mother, father, and relatives. She had hoped to continue projecting this onto her children; but this was not the approach of her second husband, so it made her sad.

Nevertheless, she showered everyone she met with the bounty of this philosophy. Everyone had value in her eyes, yet one could also still improve, she said; so she frequently—charmingly, joyously, and lovingly—gave direction and advice to one and all. We know she was very perceptive and could quickly read and assess people—assets which helped her survive the war.

We both acknowledge that our strength came from the universally known power of our loving families. This was the platform that launched us into productive and extraordinary lives. Our families projected love and the fact that we were respected as individuals. Each of us had value as a person. We were always expected to be good people because we were intrinsically worthwhile in the eyes of our families, peers, community, and God.

Safely secure in this knowledge, we were able to move through all the hardships and challenges. Though we experienced isolation and fear, we dealt with it.

Travel affected our identity, particularly our Jewish identity—a fundamental source of our legitimacy and recognition. We had to leave comfort and familiarity behind and move forward boldly; live experimentally while continuously following our hearts.

As we dictated our life stories to each other, we discussed the fact that we thought the most important factor on the immigrant road is language. Cecile's fluency in multiple languages allowed her to pass between cultures and, on many occasions, to hide in plain sight. Languages became a lifeline. We both learned to be conscious that we could be betrayed by language and accent, which sometimes makes it more difficult to blend into society. Cecile was tri-lingual, and always said that learning a language well in the country you live in is a *must*. Also, it is helpful to be in contact with someone who speaks your native language or a common language. That is what allowed us to become friends, as we had in common the French language. It provided us with a sense of security, someone we could feel close to and bounce ideas off, knowing that there is an indefinable bond. Just like family!

Living in America near Washington, DC, Cecile said, "My German accent is not a very big issue. Most people can quickly identify where I am from, thanks to Mr. Kissinger [the diplomat who was US secretary of state from 1973 to 1977]."

In my case, I still have a slight British accent with a French lilt. Very difficult to place. People are always surprised when I say I am an immigrant because I basically blend in. It is clearly documented that accents are not learned from parents but from our peers, when we are between the ages of two and five. However, accents can be acquired or lost later, as I gained and later dropped most of my British English in favor of the American words and sounds to fit in—and forgot my Arabic. In fact, as my siblings and I grew older, our parents would speak Arabic when they didn't want the children to understand what they were speaking about!

Thriving Not Just Surviving

Immigration is the engine that fuels America's growth and innovation. It allows participants to prove their mettle. Most immigrants to America have an "It can be done" attitude, so powerful and effective.

Think of all the amazing energy that immigrants bring to bear in every country they happen to go to, and the contributions they make in many fields at heights up to the Nobel Prize. This has also contributed to great changes in our society due to interracial and cross-cultural marriages.

The immigration experience has now become a phenomenon which is intensely researched and documented throughout the world. Topics explored are history, gender, culture, foods, and ethnic issues. Museums on the subject are cropping up everywhere to preserve this history and heritage, including at Ellis Island in New York.

Did Cecile and I have an identity crisis? Our answer is a resounding NO, though we experienced periods of adjustment and sometimes despondence. We shed our old selves and became free to seamlessly move into new worlds. But we needed to redefine our identity by deciding what to maintain and what to let go of. What did we need to learn? Everything: how to drive, how to shop, and how to deal with many subtle and glaring cultural differences, as well as create a whole new social group and support system. We never felt conflicted about the immigrant experience because we had already "done it," and in coming at last to America we felt that we were in a better place in our lives.

After a short introductory period, we blended easily with our new environments. We had confronted our truth with honesty and joy. It was not a barrier: we looked the truth in the eye and embraced our new identities. We are proud that we do not fit into a box, but maintained our core personalities, eclectic and diverse, and polished by encounters across the world.

Coming to a new country requires sacrifice, a lot of sacrifice. You need to immerse yourself; yet—you need to remain grounded and uncompromisingly true to your important basic values and keep faith with yourself. We had to personally discover that for ourselves.

I was and still am a nonconformist introvert who marched to a different drummer and have only a few very good friends with the same temperament.

It is odd to say, but these were some of the most productive and interesting times of my life. I learned to become a team player with my family, as we all pulled together. I learned to make do with dignity and an open mind and not feel sorry for myself. I also learned many important skills, such as sewing better, dressing well, beading, which served me well later in life.

Even as a teenage immigrant in France, my curiosity and desire to learn propelled me along. As we lived at the edge of Paris by the Porte Des Lilas Métro station, I roamed sections of the city; I became a people watcher and an observer of my surroundings, characteristics that now play a key role in my photography. I recall that when I was in middle school the teacher once asked what we had done on the previous weekend. I spoke of the many hours I had spent exploring the city, my visit to two museums (all free at the time, of course, including the Louvre), and my walking part way up the Eiffel Tower. All the students and the teacher were amazed. The teacher asked how many others had done anything like that, and several students said they had never even seen the Eiffel Tower, let alone been there. They lived a short half-hour Métro trip away. I could not believe this was the case, yet perhaps they took for granted what was so familiar to them. A missed opportunity from my point of view!

Cecile and I are also part of the Jewish people's Diaspora. We are the nomads who can be found all over this Earth. The Jews have been assets to the communities where they settled, in all areas of society: finance, commerce, education, the arts, medicine, science, etc. In America, consider the amazing contributions of Jewish immigrants in these arenas as well as in the arts, music, and particularly in Hollywood. There are Jews from Egypt all over the planet, frequently in academic fields.

We also feel we have a standard to uphold: we are expected to excel so as not to disappoint our supporting cast. We have an obligation to past generations to be productive, good citizens of whichever country we live in. This is one way of honoring them.

Sometimes religious organizations provide a safe haven and direction in time of crisis. They come to the aid of immigrants: my family took advantage of that a couple of times. Cecile was also the beneficiary of such help after the war, when she had to take care of herself and her sons.

After my family arrived in Canada, my father went to the Hebrew Immigrant Aid Society (HIAS) looking for help. They offered him all sorts of aid. He declined. He said, "Just give me enough money to buy an old car so I can get on the road and work." The society helped with money for furniture, and the car. He was over age fifty at the time, in a strange country with very cold weather, and had no connections. But he had the advantage in Quebec of speaking French as well as English. He got on the road and sold encyclopedias door to door, adding more items to his inventory when opportunities presented.

He eventually noticed that there was a paucity of French books for children in that area. With the help of his brother Maurice in France, he became the agent for Larousse, the very prestigious French publishing house, and did well selling its books.

As soon as he had made enough money, he returned the entire loan to the HIAS. They were dumbstruck. This had never happened before, he was told. He explained that by giving back the money he felt they could go on to help someone else. When our parents passed away, there was a very small sum of money left. All five siblings knew exactly what to do. We each received a very small amount as a token and the bulk of it was donated to the HIAS, which was our parents' favorite charity.

Through the years, despite assimilation, we have held onto cultural customs that keep us grounded. We have acquired friends of many backgrounds along the way, but we also have gravitated to people from our countries of origin. Diane had dear friends from Germany all of her life. I have remained close to my family and to friends from Egypt. When we are with them, we practically inhale the memories, the perfumes, and native foods with their familiar cooking aromas. The richness of those experiences can be overwhelming. I frequently prepared a Middle Eastern menu when I entertained, often by request. (That was before all these foods became mainstream and more common.) And Cecile confided, "I still like apple strudel a lot . . ."

12

Anatomy of a Friendship / Cecile and Diane

The remarkable parallels between our journeys inform the warp and weft of our friendship bond. We are sister souls. Millennials might call us BFFs. Long before our lives intersected in 1962, we walked some of the same avenues carrying the stigma of being refugees and then immigrants.

During historical upheavals, we both escaped from our countries of birth under harsh circumstances. We both became immigrants, more than once. We are both Jewish, though from different traditions and levels of participation in religious life.

We both found France a haven for refugees, and we each lived there for about ten years—never once crossing paths. Diane left France in 1959. Cecile left France in 1947. While in Paris, we both worked for the American or Allied forces or NATO as English-French translators.

Our conversations are always in French, as we seek to maintain our vocabulary and facility with this beautiful language. The dictionary is referred to frequently and as new words (such as computer—*ordinateur*) need to be learned. Our knowledge of French led us to the same career in teaching.

We're not carbon copies: Cecile loves opera and classical music. Diane enjoys them, but prefers musicals and popular music. Cecile's taste in furniture is mostly ornate, while Diane's runs to Scandinavian modern. There is nothing casual about the way we both dress: we are mostly careful about how we look.

Cecile prefers conservative suits with lovely blouses while Diane is more eclectic. As for jewelry, well, Cecile likes the traditional style, while Diane goes for artistic and unusual items. Cecile is calm, quickly assesses a situation, and makes a decision, while Diane shoots from the hip, which frequently causes problems. We obviously do not cry too much . . . We just move on. (The School of Life has taught us to be grateful, not whiners, though Diane admits to having had her share of bouts with depression.)

Although neither of us pursued an advanced degree, we have common sense and an ongoing thirst for knowledge, and have acquired a vast vocabulary. Interacting with people comes naturally to us, and we have numerous and long-lasting friendships with people of all ages and from all walks of life and places around the world.

Together, we can talk about everything and anything, as we are bound in an other-worldly way. We are spiritual seekers, art lovers, and avid readers.

Circumstances set us on the path to becoming strong, determined women. Separately, our families instilled in us "self-love," self-reliance and resourcefulness, and pride in who we are. This cornerstone of our lives allows us to be non-conformists if we so choose. We are proudly smart, brave, sophisticated, and cosmopolitan.

For more than forty-five years, our great affection for each other has been stimulated by our similar history and shared interests and passions, despite twenty years age difference and origins on different continents. Together, we have endured tests of time: illness, family crisis, children growing up, accidents. As we hit bumps in the road, we inspired each other to reach for the higher ground and strive to be better people.

13

Second Acts

"Rose Carthame," silk painting by Diane Tuckman

Retirement / Cecile

After I stopped teaching French, my life changed, again. As a retiree, I had more time to devote to my interests. Living in the Washington, DC, area, the cultural opportunities are endless. Harking back to my youth, I indulged in my love of classical music and opera.

Music has been so rewarding! I have an extensive music and opera collection, which I listen to frequently. I can easily identify which opera is playing after hearing just a few notes, as well as many other classical pieces.

Before I retired, I often went to museums and exhibitions. Nevertheless, I was limited by the fact that we had only one car and my husband was very particular about using it. I could mostly use the car in the early afternoon.

When I was young, I complained to my mother that I had no talent as an artist. Herself a talented pianist, she responded that artists in all disciplines need appreciators. So that became my role. That is what I do.

I decided to learn how to play bridge. I quickly discovered that it was not that easy! I had to learn the rules and it required concentration. I joined a group of friends and really enjoyed it. I still continue to play very occasionally, even at my age.

Being that I am a people person, I enjoyed entertaining. But that involves cooking and, as we know, *it is not my bag!* But I somehow found a way. My husband Henri also enjoyed having people over and was quite gregarious. So we organized dinner parties where I did a limited amount of cooking and preparation while Henri did most of the shopping and some cooking. My home is conducive to entertaining. We have an ornate, exquisitely carved dining room set of dark wood with leather-seated high-back chairs. The embroidered linens, beautiful china, and silverware add a touch of sophistication to the table settings. A complete silver tea set, always freshly polished, sits on the buffet. The views of the woods from the wide door and window, were always a delight. It was a nice atmosphere that encouraged great conversation particularly with wine being served!

Henri and I both enjoyed going for walks in the woods. Locally, we took long walks in Greenbelt Park behind our house. We also liked to travel. After we were introduced to a resort in the Black Forest of Germany, we went there frequently for the specific purpose of going on long walks. It brought back memories of our youth.

While in Germany, we once visited Nuremberg, my birthplace. We also often went to Florida in the winter where my cousin Margaret lived close to Palm Beach. We even took a trip to France to meet the surviving members of the Lacroix family. Everything was very different, and quite emotional.

Ah, friends! I cherish every one of them. I would make sure they were remembered on their birthdays and I would call frequently to maintain the lines of communication. I would call and so would they. Friends from different parts of the world continue to call me and fax me. But I am not of the email generation!

My sons and my grandchildren and great grandchildren are always on my mind. They play an active role in my life. My son Richard calls me every day from Arizona where he now lives.

I continue to read in English, French, and German. My husband Henri collected old books and sold two large collections to dealers. Books have always been an important part of what I do. Despite my failing vision, I still read.

I easily transitioned into a more relaxed lifestyle which has made me very happy.

Embrace the Arts / Diane

After the French teaching program ended, I was at a loose end, raising two children and looking for a new challenge. While visiting my parents in Montreal, I expressed my intention of trying something new. My father encouraged me to become the representative for a French art supply firm. My uncle Maurice in Paris became my agent. I started out selling and demonstrating the company's brilliant batik dyes.

"Family," silk painting by Diane Tuckman

In the fall of 1978, a young lady called asking to purchase dyes to paint on silk. She had been told that I was the representative for the French company. I did not know what art form she was talking about! She invited me over to see her pieces. She had spent the summer in Paris learning the art of painting on silk. I immediately knew that this was what I wanted to do.

Silk painting, as we know it today, involves techniques popularized by the French artist Litza Bain. Bringing together methods first used by French milliners, silk flower makers, and Russian artists who emigrated to France in the early part of the twentieth century, Ms. Bain combined these elements and developed a silk painting process. She started to teach the art form in the early 1960s in Paris.

I visited Litza Bain in her home studio. She had sold her business in Montmartre in Paris, right below the Sacré-Coeur, where she had started. I attended a couple of classes in her old studio, which had been taken over by

Lydie Ottelard, and was surprised as to their methodology. Very French. The participants went once a week and painted for about three hours.

In 1978, with two hundred dollars in the bank, I founded Ivy Imports (originally IV for my children's initials, but everyone always said "IVY" so that is what I changed it to). I imported silk painting products from France to launch the art of painting on silk in America, to bring the excitement of this art form to a wider audience. I was the first to import the necessary products and make them easily accessible for artists. It was very hard because very few artists in the United States knew how to use them, and those who did kept it a "deep, dark secret."

"Fire," silk painting by Diane Tuckman

I named the art form "silk painting," because during the process the dyes become one with the silk; but now it is known as "painting on silk." Silk paintings can be designed as art to hang or to be functional, such as for wearable art or home décor. Quilters, sewers, and interior and fashion designers have found painted silks very useful for their purposes.

I taught and demonstrated the art of painting on silk extensively at trade shows, conventions, and at my studio in Bladensburg, then in Beltsville, and now in Lanham, Md. Because I was in business, both my children have worked for me at some point.

A friend was helping me by painting samples. I also needed someone who knew the business of art materials to participate in art supply shows. I signed up for a convention that catered to art suppliers and applied to teach a program for individuals who worked in art supply stores. Jan Janas took the class and fell in love with the art. We bonded and have been friends and coauthors ever since. Together, we have published four books on the art of painting on silk, with the most recent in 2018.

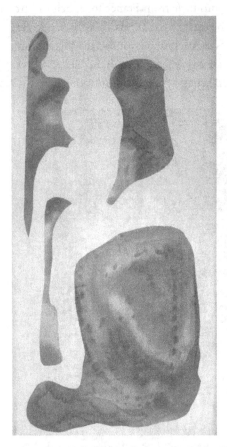

"Organic," silk painting by Diane Tuckman

The first book, *The Complete Book of Silk Painting*, sold over fifteen thousand copies. The other three also did well. Jan and I describe painting on silk this way: silk painting is a direct paint-on method. Brilliant translucent dyes are applied to the canvas, which is silk fabric, using a thrilling array of watercolor techniques. The colors merge to become an integral part of the fabric, which always remains soft to the touch. Silk painting is not static. Movement and fluidity are the hallmark of this art form. As the hand of the artist delicately or forcefully guides the flow of the liquid dyes, the colors glide through the silk and generate delight and excitement.

In 1998, as demand grew, Jan and I launched a nonprofit organization, SPIN (Silk Painters International), dedicated to bringing public awareness to silk art. I am its retired executive director. There are now five thousand silk painters connected through Facebook.

Jan and I started *The Silkworm* newsletter, which is still being published by SPIN. We organized the first biannual international silk painting festival. The festival has taken place in Virginia, Maryland, Santa Fe, and Gatlinburg (TN). Artists from all over the world attend, take classes, listen to lectures, view silk art, and participate in juried fashion and art shows.

While attempting to sell the products, I discovered that it is very difficult to establish something new. I eventually closed the import business because of debts and my lack of experience in running a business. I used to say I made several mistakes more than once. But it was a terrific experience. I learned many skills and made lifelong friends. I have continued to express my passion for the art in different ways.

Subconsciously, I always wanted to be an artist, but like most people I was gripped by the Fear of Art. My friend Jan eventually got tired of hearing me say, "I am not an artist," and really scolded me. One day, during one of her classes, she ordered me to paint. Now I can proudly say—and it easily rolls off my tongue—"I am an artist."

"Flying Guitars," photograph by Diane Tuckman

While all this was going on, I also became a florist, took many classes, and did custom work, weddings, and special events. I retired from this endeavor.

I continue to create. I've organized juried silk art exhibitions in museums and other venues. I have a studio where I have taught silk art and completed commissions. My background as a teacher certainly did not hurt! I also lectured on the subject in many different venues, and offered hands-on demonstrations in museums and elsewhere. Very recently, I gave a workshop at the Jewish Museum of Maryland in Baltimore, where my work is sold in the museum gift shop.

My greatest joy is to introduce people to painting on silk. My pleasure is when they apply brush to silk and I see their amazement and delight. When students surpass their teacher, it is the best compliment.

"Tree of Life," silk painting with stitching, by Diane Tuckman

I am also a photographer. I show my work in many different venues and by invitation. I am proud of my work in this field. I have participated in several large shows and some solo shows. With this medium, I attempt to catch "the moment," beautiful or interesting. All my life experiences inform my photography.

I was constantly supported and encouraged by my friend Cecile in my artistic endeavors.

Epilogue / Diane

The Foundation of Our Faith

We are seekers and storytellers.

When our families fled persecution, we took with us our faith and our faith in ourselves. We learned to trust our instincts, which aided us again and again in our journeys as immigrants. Both our families, in different ways, instilled in us a very strong Jewish identity, which was indestructible and could not be shaken despite the many trials and tribulations and the seduction of assimilation.

As we mentioned earlier, we are originally from different continents, cultures, and eras. We share many things; an important one is that we are unequivocally Jewish. Cecile is Ashkenazi and Diane is Sephardic, with many basic ideas in common and some traditions that diverge. Still, Jewish people-hood is our bedrock. We definitely consider ourselves to be members of the group MOTT, as they say—Members of the Tribe. Our faith is for us a frame of reference—it calls to us to be witnesses. We are part of the narrative.

Spirituality implies a set of conventions. We view it more as a guiding framework. Religion for us is a frame of reference: it calls to us to be witnesses as we experienced high human dramas, now recalled from the depths as memories and emotions, probably enhanced by imagination and time.

We both try to adhere to some Jewish principles: respect for the world and living things, seasonal thanks for the harvests and life cycles. Nature speaks to us and has affected our lives—beach sand between our toes, sometimes sand between our teeth during sandstorms, the shelter and the shadows of forests, the rivers, seas, and amazing landscapes of our travels.

We never believed in victimhood but considered ourselves to be survivors. We did not wait for Moses to take us to the Promised Land, yet somehow we found our way there—to America . . .

"I do not want to dwell on the Holocaust, the loss of my family, my first husband, my difficult life, and the aftermath," Cecile said. "I prefer to focus positively on the people who sheltered me and my children, befriended me, and helped me."

As we dictated our life stories to each other, we recorded not just memories but observations. We took time to question, debate, and probe our recollections for meaning and lessons. In hindsight, we see that not all of our questions have answers, but the questions themselves are worthy. Chronicling each other's journeys revealed parallels in our immigrant experiences that inform the anatomy of our special friendship. Among the greatest values we found there was spirituality.

Spirituality resonates with a profound vibration that you cannot see, just feel. We agree that being MINDFUL in everything we do, down to the mundane, is a good trait.

Cecile once said: "We are sometimes called the Chosen People. Are we chosen to suffer? Is that the source of age-old and persistent hatred?" We ponder that, while personally attempting to live honorable lives.

We feel that with the privilege of being Jewish comes a responsibility. To face life with indomitable spirit is a gift, based on the ability of our forebearers to persistently survive in the face of adversity. They had courage, audacity, grit, and grace. Therefore, to express our admiration and to honor them we continue the traditions. They taught us valuable lessons, such as the importance of education, caring for all people, and being good citizens in whichever country we landed in. Therefore, we acknowledge that in Jewish tradition it is important to contribute to all fields of knowledge and make financial contributions to social programs for the betterment of mankind.

We have had many experiences with premonitions. Our goal has been to take charge of these premonitions and act on them if we feel that they are right for us at that moment.

Admitting that we are not perfect is very powerful, but we must continue to strive. Both of us, when we sometimes feel down, will hear something that tells us it is time to raise ourselves up again and move forward.

We have been empowered by our personal inner strength and by many kind people around us. As we traveled, even when we had few material things, our baggage was transportable: we carried the love and admiration of our parents.

We experienced much wickedness and much kindness.

We continue to boldly wrestle with the mysteries of life. Where is the Divine in the equation? It is everywhere and in everything we think, do, and don't do. Are things preordained? We discuss and struggle with this issue.

We can make a difference in the world with our involvement, especially in a selfless way. Through the Jewish concept of "repairing the world" we try to reach out to the outstretched hands.

Asking and giving forgiveness, which we do on Yom Kippur, is a powerful Jewish concept. We ask forgiveness from people we have offended or hurt during that year so that we can then ask for forgiveness from God. We need to ask that person three times for forgiveness. If they do not offer forgiveness, we are considered to be exonerated and move on. God is a participant in what good we can do within the power of deep-seated hope. Divine Love—Being Alive is good. We are all DIVINELY interconnected.

We feel we are citizens of the human race. With all the current globalization, our multi-country experiences allow us to feel comfortable and open with people from various cultures.

Our Jewish identity surfaces in moments of crisis. In our quest, we seek answers to the universal questions. We ponder the mystery of spirituality beyond religion.

We rejoice and celebrate, regardless of our pasts. We seek wisdom in all its forms—a tough journey.

We tried to hone our qualities of listening, noticing, and paying attention. We feel a great level of spontaneity in our lives.

We are delighted that women have found such freedom, particularly in America. We have seen the great successes achieved by the feminist revolution—the great strides in women's rights and the redefinition of our role in society. Many cultures are still struggling with these issues. As history has shown, in all societies the lives of children and most other individuals are positively impacted by improvements in women's conditions. All women are climbing up the ladder on the shoulders of other brave women. We salute their achievements, fully realizing it is a work in progress.

It is important that we, in some ways, captured our childhoods in a spontaneous way, and did not forget. Revisiting it has been nurturing. Some parts of our childhoods were remarkable.

We have an unflagging determination in all we do. We even look to deal with evil, a human condition and battle between good and evil.

What did we run away from? What did we embrace? We turned inward to access our strengths.

We questioned: Where is home anymore? Where do I fit? But we both kept moving forward, finding our places in this new society.

We consider ourselves citizens of the PLANET, yet privileged to be Americans.

There were times when we were SUSPENDED in disbelief (internally) as to what was happening to us, yet grounded in the reality of the events and shared experiences.

To be a displaced person was a privilege; it brought out the best in us. Out of suffering came redemption for us.

At times, we felt a sense of abandonment, loss, and darkness as we moved through our travails. Nevertheless, due to our temperaments and the teachings and values of our families and ancestors, we carried on with a sense of determination: we had reality to deal with.

Friendship played a very big role in our lives, as we leaned on friends and family to help us through difficult times and losses, and to celebrate joys. As we endured the health issues that come with age, we did not have to suffer alone. We had family and friends to empathize, and we felt a strong connection and help from the Divine. We felt the Love, as well as the connecting force with people directed to us.

Are events a gift? We ponder. Is it uncanny luck? Not by choice but by Divine interference. We think about that and all the unusual interconnections in our lives.

In some ways, these were the most productive times in our lives. We learned great and wonderful things. We coped, learned skills, and grew spiritually as we developed our personal philosophies.

Our prayers have expressed hope, in our tradition, for a better world.

WE GIVE THANKS FOR OUR ANCESTORS, THE PRIVILEGE OF LIFE, WONDERS OF NATURE, OUR FAITH, OUR SOCIETY, AS WE ASPIRE TO BECOMING BETTER INDIVIDUALS.

To My German Friends / Cecile

It is highly ironic that I now have many good German friends. After all I went through, this is difficult for most people to understand—particularly my children.

This is how it came about.

My husband Henri and I met Dr. Fritz Karl Mann. He was a professor of economics at George Washington University. We came to meet him because Henri was in the same academic field. Dr. Mann left Germany very early and came here when he was offered a teaching position.

He entertained frequently, hosting people from different countries and backgrounds. This is where Henri and I met several Germans who were extraordinarily nice and somehow became our good friends. Of course, we had an affinity for each other—a common language and cultural background. They were all economists, but from a younger generation. We never discussed the history of Germany.

These friends encouraged us to go back to Germany for a visit.

Dr. Mann would go to a *pension* at the edge of the Black Forest and always raved about the area. So we finally went.

We found the area to be quite lovely; the *pension* was right at the edge of the forest with many trails for long walks. At the time, Henri and I enjoyed walking, so this was a perfect vacation for us. It reminded me of growing up in Germany, when walking was a way of life.

We went to the same place about five times as we found it convenient and restful. We met and became very friendly with a couple, and eventually with their daughter Amerei and her husband Horst Zimmerman and Amerei's parents; the Zimmermans frequently came to spend time with us when we were at the *pension*. We also met another couple, the Henkes. Through Amerei's parents, we met the Glazers. I am still very good friends with all of them. The Glazers and I have developed a very close relationship because they lived in Washington for quite a long time and came frequently for health reasons.

All in all, my friendships with the Glazers and the Zimmermans have continued to flourish.

Postscript and Acknowledgments

Postscript

On September 21, 2010, Cecile passed away. She was buried next to Henri in Maryland in a military cemetery (although he was born in Germany, he became a US citizen and later a veteran). Diane arranged for a memorial plaque placed in the Mishkan Torah synagogue in Greenbelt, where Cecile finally found her Jewish spiritual home and community. There, Diane lights a Yahrzeit candle every year on the anniversary of her death. "It is now my turn to continue our legacy," Diane says, in keeping her promise to complete their dual memoir.

Cecile's 90th birthday party

Through research after WWII, Cecile learned that Julius Wasserman, the first love of her life and father of her sons, was murdered in the Shoah, near Kaunas, Lithuania, year and exact location unknown.

Diane's husband, Morton, passed away in 2015 after a long illness.

Acknowledgments—Cecile Spiegel

To my sons, Marc Robert and Claude Richard. They saved me and they saved us, more than once. I was pregnant with Robert and therefore I was one of the few persons let go from a roundup of German Jewish women at the Velodrome d'Hiver in Paris. Also, because Richard was under age two in 1944, and not eligible to be deported, we were all three temporarily saved.

To the many Righteous Ones: the French Ambassador to England, the Lacroix family, and all of the Righteous anonymous and named individuals from France who helped and befriended me along the way, even some German soldiers.

Acknowledgments—Diane Tuckman

To Cecile, who would say of our age difference, with a twinkle in her piercing blue eyes, "I could be your mother, you know!" I would look at her and we would burst out laughing. We were more like sisters, yet her motherly advice was always there when needed. Cecile was ninety years old when we launched into the memoir project in 2005. She participated in creating the manuscript's first draft, but left us in 2010 before the book was completed. Cecile wanted her story to be told, so I have done my best to finish the task we embarked on together. I know that she will continue to watch over me, advise me, and keep me on the straight and narrow.

To my family, who empowered me to complete this book and constantly help me to reach my goals. My siblings Gisele, Alain, Joyce, and Danny tolerated my continuous questioning as I looked for authenticity and veracity for this book. They shared many memories and perspectives. Joyce gave us a valuable title for this book, translated various documents into French, and contributed incisive texts to the manuscript.

Anatomy of a Friendship bridges the past and the present trajectory of our lives. When Cecile and I launched into our memoir I was initially reluctant to tackle such a personal and difficult project, even though I had written several art books. Over lunch, I asked my friend Judith Friedenberg, a professor and a published author, for her advice as to whom I should tap for help. She looked me straight in the eye and said, "Only YOU can do it!" She laid out some suggestions and told me to GO FOR IT . . . And we did. Judith, thank you.

Jennifer Gillispie also told me that this was a very personal project, and no one else could give it the credence and context as well as we could. Jennifer, thank you.

To Daria Semchenkova, for her many excellent suggestions and for bringing order from chaos with the manuscript.

To Jean Thompson, our first editor, who said, "I would be honored to work on this interesting project." For her extensive knowledge as an editor, her faith in the project, her keen eye, and her dedication, I am most thankful. She interviewed Cecile and me at length. We started this odyssey by using our notes and stories. I had been thinking about this book and was very concerned that I did not have the skills to weave the stories into a readable manuscript. The day I met

Jean Thompson was momentous! Over the years, she has been with us every step of the way, bringing her clear vision and amazing editorial skills. Here is a thank you for her great contributions.

To countless historical and cultural resources that helped illuminate the Heliopolis of my childhood and the political and cultural backdrops of our immigration journeys, including the French Embassy in Washington, DC, the US Holocaust Museum, the Yad Vashem Archives in Jerusalem, and various books on the Egyptian Jewish diaspora, Germany, France, etc.

To all my friends including Idaz Greenberg, Constance Battle, Jan Janas, Sue Laden, and Dr. Julie Rosenberg, who encouraged me to complete the project so I could acknowledge the role Cecile played in our lives. This poem reflects my deep friendship with Cecile: she is my sister soul.

Cecile at home in Lanham, MD

Friendship

GREAT FRIENDSHIP IS A BLESSING, RARE, PRECIOUS AND FRAGILE
I looked into her twinkling blue eyes and saw a sister soul!
We connected and became lifelong close friends and confidantes.
We Listened PATIENTLY, stopped to think and then spoke . . .
We finished each other's sentences.
The advice flowed easily with a smile and a thank you! It was taken and acted on.
We traveled a long road together with love, respect, and affection.
Great memories were created
But . . . even a firm strong friendship, though fleeting, is a precious and rare gift.

—Diane Tuckman, 2019
Lanham, MD

Timeline

Year	Cecile Steinhard Wasserman Spiegel	Diane Yedid Tuckman
1914		Egypt, which has been occupied by the British since 1882, is declared a British protectorate.
1915	Born in Nuremberg, Germany.	
1919	Peace settlement ending WWI. The German Workers' Party (DAP) emerges; opposed to the settlement, and espousing German supremacy and antisemitism, it will later become the Nazi Party.	
1922		Treaty of alliance gives Egypt independence, but with continued British presence.
1923	First of many Nazi rallies occurs in Nuremberg. These soon become massive, annual propaganda events.	
1932	Father dies. Cecile takes a job and experiences anti-Jewish harassment.	
1933	Moves to Munich with mother. Hitler becomes German Chancellor.	
1934	Hitler becomes Germany's Fuhrer. Mother decides Cecile must leave country. Cecile's fiance, Julius, has already fled to England.	

1935	Sails for London, England.	Born in Heliopolis, Egypt.
1936	Moves to Paris to join Julius.	
1939	WWII begins.	
	Flees to the countryside after bombs fall on Paris.	
1940	France surrenders to German forces and is partitioned into occupied and free zones. British Commonwealth forces battle Italian Fascist forces in North Africa.	
1941	US declares war on the Axis powers. Nazi German forces enter North Africa.	
1943	German and Italian forces surrender in North Africa.	
1945	WWII ends.	
	With her children, Cecile makes way back to Paris.	In Egypt, tensions continue related to Britain's influence on the monarchy and on affairs in the Middle East. Nationalists organize in Egypt.
1947	Relatives in New Jersey, USA, sponsor Cecile and her children to emigrate. Soon after, she marries and moves to Maryland suburbs of Washington, DC.	
1948		Palestine is divided into a Jewish state and an Arab state. In May 1948, first Arab-Israeli War begins. In Egypt, tensions rise. Zionists are rounded up. Jews in Heliopolis report harassment and assaults. Family flees to Italy then settles in Paris.

1952		The Egyptian monarchy is overthrown by nationalist politicians led by Gamel Abdel Nasser.
1959		In Paris, works as a translator and typist for the American military and meets her future husband. Moves from Paris to Montreal, and then to the US.
1962	Diane and Cecile meet in a Maryland training program for teachers of French.	

CPSIA information can be obtained
at www.ICGtesting.com
Printed in the USA
JSHW011600030822
28820JS00002B/27